Baseball Puzzles

Word Finds, Crosswords, Trivia, and More

By Stephen Bratkovich

Published by IngramSpark LLC
LaVergne, TN 37086

ISBN 979-8-9860103-4-2

DEDICATION

To Emily

with Love and Many Thanks

CONTENTS

CONTENTS

CONTENTS

Late Innings

CONTENTS

Extra Innings

CONTENTS

INTRODUCTION

Are you ready to challenge your brain on baseball knowledge? Do you have your thinking cap by your side? Are your pencils sharp and ready to go? If so, read on, and dive into puzzles, trivia, word finds, crosswords, and minutiae on America's National Pastime.

A decision that had to be made from the infancy of this project was, "What source will be used for the myriad of answers to all of the baseball questions?" Thankfully, a reliable source is readily available in Baseball-Reference which can be found at https://www.baseball-reference.com. Unless otherwise noted, all answers to questions are from this source. The years from 1901 through the 2022 season were used. And, questions and answers refer to Major League Baseball (MLB).

A disclaimer: Questions, and answers, were compiled at the completion of the 2022 MLB season. Negro League statistics are not included in this document. Updates and future editions will include **all** major leagues.

Some questions have an imposed time limit. Apologies to those with "time phobia," medically called chronophobia (extreme fear of the passage of time). Take as much time as you want with these questions!

Questions are rated by difficulty starting with **Single** (lowest level), and progressing to **Double**, **Triple**, and **Home Run** (highest/most difficult level). Also, the level on some questions is "multiple," indicating you can decide on the difficulty level you want to tackle (**SINGLE** to **HOME RUN**). And, this is important (at least to the author), the **SINGLE, DOUBLE, TRIPLE** and **HOME RUN** levels, are assigned with the assumption that friends, baseball gurus, books, internet searches, etc., are off limits in seeking answers to questions. In other words, use the knowledge in your brain and not the brain of someone else.

The outline of the book is in four parts:

Early Innings — Middle Innings — Late Innings — Extra Innings

The "Early Innings" section has more than half of the questions in the **SINGLE/DOUBLE** difficulty levels. The questions in the "Middle/Late Innings" sections are progressively more difficult than "Early Innings." The questions in "Extra Innings" are the most difficult (many **HOME RUN** level questions).

A suggestion for readers: Start with a few of the "Early Innings" questions. If the questions are on par with your knowledge of baseball, then continue with this section. However, if you have little difficulty with "Early Innings," then move on to "Middle Innings," or even "Late Innings." "Extra Innings" should be done last, or your brain might need scheduling for continuous whirlpool treatment or a lengthy massage!

Note: Some questions have more than one correct answer, such as, "Name two right fielders that are in the Baseball Hall of Fame (HOF)? Reggie **Jackson** and Hank **Aaron** are correct answers. However, Reggie **Jackson** and Roberto **Clemente** are <u>also</u> correct answers, as are **Aaron** and **Clemente**. After each chapter, the '"answer" given to this type of question is merely one possible solution. If this sounds confusing, hang in there, as the "more than one correct answer" questions should become clear as you move through the pages.

As noted earlier, many answers can be found on baseball-reference.com. Therefore, "looking up the answer" is a relatively easy, and quick task (especially when website navigation is mastered). In essence, answers to questions are on the "honor system," and to test your knowledge of Major League Baseball. And remember, questions and answers are from 1901 through 2022.

Good Luck!

1

EARLY INNINGS

1. LEVEL: SINGLE

TAKE ME OUT TO THE BALL GAME . . . was written by Jack Norworth and composed by Albert Von Tilzer in 1908. The song is considered one of the best known and most played U.S. songs.[1]

Take this short quiz and find out how well you know the song's chorus. Get all the answers correct and run to 1st base with a **SINGLE**.

Chorus for Take Me Out to the Ball Game

Take me out to the ball game,
Take me out with the crowd.
Buy __(1)__ some __(2)__ and cracker jack,
I don't care if I __(3)__ get back,
Let __(4)__ root, root, root for the home team,
If __(5)__ don't win it's a shame.
For it's one, two, three strikes, you're out,
At the __(6)__ ball game.

1. ________________   4. ________________

2. ________________   5. ________________

3. ________________   6. ________________

WORD FIND - 3,000 Hit Club . . . As of the 2022 Major League Baseball (MLB) season, only 33 players (from a total of more than 20,000 MLB players) have achieved the feat of 3,000 or more career base hits.[2] The Word Find below contains the last name of 15 of the 33 "3,000 Hit Club" players. Can you find all 15 players?

Find the name in the puzzle.
Words can go in any direction and share letters as they cross over each other.

```
T  E  F  T  S  N  W  N  I  W
S  T  S  R  O  S  E  N  R  E
W  Y  E  R  B  G  R  Y  O  S
N  O  A  R  E  N  A  W  T  O
X  A  O  M  B  E  C  G  I  Q
K  C  W  I  N  F  I  E  L  D
K  T  I  I  C  S  G  G  O  B
E  O  L  A  I  S  U  M  M  V
G  A  E  T  N  E  M  E  L  C
K  L  C  O  B  B  H  O  I  N
```

AARON	BOGGS	BRETT
BROCK	CAREW	CLEMENTE
COBB	GWYNN	KALINE
MAYS	MOLITOR	MUSIAL
ROSE	WANER	WINFIELD

3. LEVEL: DOUBLE

ANAGRAMS . . . The letters of each MLB player's <u>last</u> name in this list can be rearranged in multiple ways to form other words. I provide the name; your job is to come up with <u>one</u> anagram of <u>all</u> the letters in the given (last) name of the player. For example: The letters in the name "Carter" can be rearranged to spell "crater" (or "tracer").

Solve these five questions/anagrams in under four minutes and you can rest while standing on second base with a **DOUBLE**.

Babe **RUTH**   _____________________

Duke **SNIDER**   _____________________

Mike **TROUT**   _____________________

Trea **TURNER**   _____________________

Corey **SEAGER** _____________________

4. LEVEL: DOUBLE

HOME RUNS R US . . . Name four (4) of the top five all-time home run hitters in Major League Baseball (MLB) history (HR Totals NOT required!).

_____________________   _____________________

_____________________   _____________________

5. LEVEL: SINGLE

JOE . . . In my family, "Joe" (Joseph) is a very common name. In fact, I had/have seven (7) relatives named Joe just on my father's side of the family (first-cousins, uncles, and grandfather). Likewise, Joe is a common name of MLB players (more so in the past). How many MLB players named "Joe" can you list in 1 minute? (I provide one to get you started).

DiMaggio

6. LEVEL: SINGLE

A, B, C . . . Can you list ten items/events that you might see at a MLB game in A, B, C order; i.e., first item/event begins with the letter "A," second item/event begins with the letter "B," and so forth? The items or events can be on the playing field, in the crowd, or anywhere in the stadium. An answer for "A" is given as a bonus to you. (Complete in 90 seconds for a **SINGLE**).

A.   <u>   Argument   </u>

B.   __________________

C.   __________________

D.   __________________

E.   __________________

F.   __________________

G.   __________________

H.   __________________

I.   __________________

J.   __________________

7. LEVEL: MULTIPLE

I AM . . . This is a puzzler where you need to answer a question with a player name, team, or town/state. Get 9 - 10 questions correct and you just hit a **HOME RUN**; 7 to 8 correct earns you a **TRIPLE**; 5 to 6 correct is a **DOUBLE**, and 3 to 4 correct is worth a line drive **SINGLE**.

1. I am the all-time MLB base hits leader. ________________________

2. I am the first player to hit 715 HRs in MLB. ________________________

3. I am the record holder with 7 MLB no-hitters in a career from 1966-93. ________________________.

4. I am the "fire-baller" from Iowa who pitched for Cleveland. ________________________

5. I am the NY Giant who made the great World Series catch in 1954. ________________________

6. I am the player who has the pitching award named after me. ________________________

7. I am the midwestern team that has appeared in the most World Series other than the Yankees. ________________________

8. I am the town and state where the Baseball Hall of Fame and Museum is located. ________________________, ________________________

9. I am the first MLB player to hit 60 HRs in one season. ________________________

10. I am the MLB player who won 9 consecutive batting average titles in the early 20th Century. ________________________

8. LEVEL: HOME RUN

WORD TOWER . . . Every word in a word tower begins with the same two letters. You build the tower by increasing the length of each word by one letter. For example, a tower on letters CA could include: CAp (3 letters), CAll (4 letters), CAtch (5 letters), etc.

Let's see how far you can go on a "baseball stadium theme" (i.e., all words must be something one could find/related to a baseball game held in a MLB stadium). (*Note: Proper nouns are not allowed, and you can't just add an s to the underline next word in your tower. For example, if your three-letter word is "hit," your four-letter word cannot be "hits." You can only use "hits" if the word directly proceeding it was NOT "hit.")* For a big (**Home Run**) challenge, get to "tower-level 10" in four minutes.

Baseball Stadium Theme—first two letters: BA

    1.   BA ___

    2.   BA ___ ___

    3.   BA ___ ___ ___

    4.   BA ___ ___ ___ ___

    5.   BA ___ ___ ___ ___ ___

    6.   BA ___ ___ ___ ___ ___ ___

    7.   BA ___ ___ ___ ___ ___ ___ ___

    8.   BA ___ ___ ___ ___ ___ ___ ___ ___

    9.   BA ___ ___ ___ ___ ___ ___ ___ ___ ___

    10.   BA ___ ___ ___ ___ ___ ___ ___ ___ ___ ___

9. LEVEL: DOUBLE

HIDDEN NAMES . . . This puzzle involves finding a last name of a MLB player that is hidden somewhere in the sentence. The correct answer could be spread over one, two, or several words. All punctuation, capital letters, etc., should be ignored when searching for the hidden name. For example, the sentence: [A true hero seldom seeks glory] contains the last name of a famous MLB player, Pete **Rose**. Do you see it? [A true he**ro se**ldom seeks glory]. (A clue is provided after each sentence)

Can you find the hidden MLB player names (last names) in the following sentences?

1. The jet erred in ignoring flight control. _______________ (Clue: Hall of Fame Shortstop)

2. The airplane flew over land erratically but surprisingly passed perfectly over water bodies. _______________ (Clue: Pitcher drafted by the Tigers in 2004)

3. The Milwaukee "Brew Crew" hit eight consecutive singles in one game. _______________ (Clue: A color)

4. The doctor reviewed her charts once a day. ___________ (Clue: Former Yankees manager)

5. From bear and caribou to newts and salamanders, U.S. forests are quite diverse. _______________ (Clue: *Ball Four* book)

6. The use of correct spelling and proper grammar is a necessity for newspaper columnists. _______________ (Clue: 1961)

7. The recipe called for cilantro, utilizing the herb as a garnish to the dish. _________ (Clue: Centerfielder who won NL Rookie of the Year Award in 2012)

8. The denial on software purchases was infuriating to the engineers. ___________ (Clue: First Baseman and winner of Home Run Hitting Contest prior to All-Star game)

9. For Bob, the native Afghanistan "tongue" was as difficult for him to learn as Polish or Ukrainian. _____________ (Clue: Home Run hitter who debuted with Florida in 2010)

10. The wild bronco leapt, kicked, and reared up on his hind legs whenever anyone tried to ride him. __________________ (Clue: Pitcher born in California and attended UCLA)

10. LEVEL: TRIPLE

WHAT'S IN THERE? . . . For this puzzler, the player name will be provided. Your job is to take the last two letters of the last name, reverse the order of the letters, and begin a new word of something you might find in a MLB dugout. Clear as the mud on a rain-out game?

An example should clarify the task: Josh Willingham played 11 seasons in MLB. In 2012 he hit 35 HRs and drove in 110 runs (both career highs) for the Minnesota Twins. The last two letters of Willingh<u>am</u> are A and M. Reversing the two letters results in M and A. Can you think of what might be in a MLB dugout that begins with the first two letters of M and A? Of course, the answer is <u>MA</u>NAGER.

Player names, that begin with MA (for the example just given), like Machado, Marichal, Maddox, Mantle, etc., are NOT allowed. However, allowable answers include team names (like Cubs, Dodgers, etc.), objects used in the playing of a baseball game (bats, balls, gloves, etc.), items used by players before or during the game (batting tees, pine tar, gum, Gatorade, etc.), player positions (pitcher, catcher, etc.), non-player personnel (manager, coach, etc.), and other items or people that could be found in a MLB dugout.

Now it's your turn. Here are the MLB names.

Clayton **Kershaw** (active in 2022)   1. _______________________

Francisco **Lindor** (active in 2022)   2. _______________________

Jim Ray **Hart** (1963 - 1974)   3. _______________________

Dave **Stieb** (1979 – 1998)   4. _______________________

Sammy **Sosa** (1989 – 2007)   5. _______________________

Jim **Adduci** (2013 – 2019)[3]   6. _______________________

Chipper **Jones** (1993 – 2012)   7. _______________________

Dick **Groat** (1952 – 1967)   8. _______________________

Sonny **Gray** (active in 2022)   9. _______________________

Larry **Elliot** (1962 - 1966)   10. _______________________

(Note: More than a dozen "Elliot(t)'s" played in MLB, but only Larry spelled his last name with one "t.")

11. LEVEL: TRIPLE

CROSS OUT . . . In the grid below are MLB player names, numbers, baseball terms, adverbs, adjectives, and so forth. Follow the directions to reveal a secret sentence.

Directions:

1. Cross out all <u>pitchers</u>.

2. Cross out all <u>adverbs</u> and <u>adjectives</u>.

3. Cross out all players who were primarily <u>right fielders</u>.

4. Cross out all abbreviations (acronyms) <u>NOT</u> related to baseball.

5. Cross out all <u>even</u> numbers.

6. Cross out all <u>objects</u> pertaining to the playing of baseball.

7. Cross out all players who were primarily <u>center fielders</u>.

8. <u>Unscramble </u>all remaining terms to reveal the secret sentence.

9. Secret Sentence____.

Mickey Mantle	Slow	Helmet	High	573
Home Runs	Speedy	714	Roger Clemens	Hank Aaron
Warren Spahn	Bat	Ty Cobb	Ball	NFL
Roberto Clemente	536	Juan Marichal	Harmon Killebrew	512
510	Agile	Hit	56	Fast
Joe DiMaggio	MLB	Willie Mays	Justin Verlander	NHL

12. LEVEL: DOUBLE

ONE LETTER AT A TIME . . . Go from the top word to the bottom word by changing only one letter and forming a common English word at each step. You can't change the letter's order. Here's an example.

To go from TAGS to OUTS, a possible solution is shown, with the one letter changed <u>underlined</u>:

TAGS

<u>B</u>AGS   (The T has been changed to a B)
B<u>U</u>GS   (The A has been changed to a U)
BU<u>T</u>S   (The G has been changed to a T)

<u>O</u>UTS   (The B has been changed to an O)

Clues are provided to help you solve the puzzle. Note: Baseball terms/ words are not required when a letter is changed.

If you're successful in going from BUNT to WALK, then slide into second with a 2-Bagger (**DOUBLE**).

B U N T

________   (type of bed)

________   (a large mass)

________   (illegal move in baseball)

W A L K

13. LEVEL: MULTIPLE

THE KEY IS . . . Many MLB players over the years had short 3-letter names. How many can you list in <u>three minutes</u>? (NOTE: Same spelling of a last name only counts as ONE last name). I'll give you one 3-letter name to start you off.

> If you get 5-9 names, you hit a **SINGLE**.
> For 10-12 names, a stand-up **DOUBLE**.
> For listing 13-15 names, you slugged a **TRIPLE**.
> For 15+ names, "touch 'em all" for a **HOME RUN**!

Jimmy **KEY** ____

____

____

____

14. LEVEL: DOUBLE

RHYME TIME . . . Each clue leads to a 2-word answer that rhymes, such as FLAT BAT or BALK TALK. The numbers in parentheses after the clue give the number of letters in each word of the answer. For example, "a long home run by center fielder and All-Star Mike T. (5, 5)" would be "Trout clout."

1. Diminutive home run barrier (5, 4) _______ _______

2. Ball in the dirt (3, 5) _______ _______

3. An error by the home team at Wrigley (3, 4) _______ _______

4. A cold Mays in center field (6, 6) _______ _______

5. Nickname of MLB team from Wisconsin (4, 4) _______ _______

6. Former NY manager Torre's tootsies (4, 4) (pl.) _______ _______

7. Pitcher Vida's footwear (5, 5) (pl.) _______ _______

15. LEVEL: TRIPLE

MATH . . . Here are a couple puzzlers to test your math skills. (Don't worry, I won't tell your former math teacher how you did!). Get both answers correct and slide into third with a **TRIPLE.**

1. Joe and Jerry have been running first and second place all season in the race for Batting Average (BA) title. Joe finished the season with a .339 BA. Jerry finished the season with 175 base hits in 510 "official" at-bats. Who won the batting average title, Joe or Jerry, <u>and</u>, what was their batting average?

   Winner _________________   Batting Average _______

2. A baseball game was viewed by 40,007 fans, minus the square root of 81, plus three. What was the attendance? ____________

16. LEVEL: SINGLE

LE . . . All of the answers in this puzzler are "items" or "events" that you might see at a ball game, <u>and</u> contain the consecutive letters LE. The LE can be at the beginning, end, or somewhere "inside" the word. For example, if the clue was, "The last game of a series," the answer would be "finaLE."

1. A two-base hit. ____________________

2. A player edging off a base. ____________________

3. The fourth hitter in a line-up is usually known by this moniker. ____________________

4. The number "7" player if you're keeping score. ____________________

5. The thin part of a bat. ____________________

6. To jump up for a ball. ____________________

7. A "way" to commit an error on, or misplay, a ground ball. ____________________

8. A "southpaw" pitcher ____________________

9. The term for a one-base hit, double, triple, and home run by one player in one game. ____________________

10. The "past tense" of swiping a base. ____________________

17. LEVEL: DOUBLE

A HIDDEN BASEBALL WORD . . . Can you find the one "baseball" word (Out, Error, and Walk are three examples) that is hidden somewhere in the sentences below? The correct answer could be spread over one, two, or several words. Ignore all punctuation, capital letters, etc., when looking for the hidden baseball word.

An example is the sentence: The dark shadows and starry sky indicated it was night again. The answer is tag. Do you see it? [The dark shadows and starry sky indicated it was nigh**t ag**ain.]

The answers to the questions are six of the 12 words below:

slide	catch	triple	throw
safe	save	score	bat
team	run	win	ball

1. At the yard sale, the woman bought a baby crib, a table, and a sofa. ___________________

2. Intrigued by the colorful window, I never would have thought it was made from plastic. ___________________

3. Due to lack of a breeze and shallow water depth, rowing the sailboat to shore was the only option for the couple. ___________________

4. When "Mensa" verified, and then supported, Ralph's calculation, the city council rapidly approved the proposal. ___________________

5. Was the house with the haunted attic at Church Street or 5th? ___________________

6. Ivan and Dimitri pleaded with customs officials to reopen their case files. ___________________

18. LEVEL: MULTIPLE

ONE-SYLLABLE BASEBALL . . . How many one-syllable baseball terms (words) can you come up with in <u>one minute</u>? (I provided two terms/ words to get you started which count toward your total).

20+ terms –	**HOME RUN**
17-20 terms –	**TRIPLE**
14-16 terms –	**DOUBLE**
Up to 13 terms –	**SINGLE**

<u> bat   ball </u> ______ ______ ______ ______ ______ ______ ______ ______

______ ______ ______ ______ ______ ______ ______ ______

19. LEVEL: SINGLE

WORD FIND - 2016 CUBS . . . In 2016, the Chicago Cubs ended a drought that extended more than a century. In 1908, the Cubs won the World Series. One-hundred eight years had passed before the Cubs, and their "bleed Cubbie blue fans" could again claim to be champions of the world.

In the "word find" on the next page are the names of 15 players from the 2016 championship team. Some players participated in a majority of the games, some played in far fewer. Regardless, they all can proudly exclaim, "2016 Champions."

Circle, underline, or mark the player names. You can check your answers at the chapter's end.

Find the name in the puzzle.

Words can go in any direction and share letters as they cross over each other.

2016 WORLD SERIES CHAMPION CHICAGO CUBS

```
A  J  L  B  M  J  F  M  M  D  I  R
Y  L  A  A  L  X  O  J  S  Z  S  E
L  E  M  F  C  N  T  N  A  Y  R  B
Z  L  H  O  T  K  R  K  E  L  A  R
A  Y  E  E  R  E  E  T  R  E  V  A
R  N  R  S  L  A  S  Y  T  S  Q  W
R  O  A  W  S  I  Y  E  N  T  P  H
I  D  O  M  R  U  P  Q  O  E  J  C
E  F  E  B  P  R  R  E  C  R  C  S
T  Q  O  F  Z  A  V  H  D  B  H  Z
A  Z  Q  N  E  C  H  O  Z  Z  I  R
H  E  Y  W  A  R  D  C  U  W  A  W
```

ALMORA	ARRIETA	BAEZ	BRYANT	CHAPMAN
CONTREAS	FOWLER	HEYWARD	LACKEY	LESTER
MONTERO	RIZZO	RUSSELL	SCHWARBER	ZOBRIST

20. LEVEL: MULTIPLE

MATCH 'EM . . . Many MLB players have been born outside the U.S. See if you can identify the player in the following list with his home country.

Up to 3 correct: **SINGLE**
4-5 correct: **DOUBLE**
6-7 correct: **TRIPLE**
8-10 correct: **HOME RUN**

1.	Orlando Cepeda	______	a. Japan
2.	Jose Altuve	______	b. Mexico
3.	Bert Blyleven	______	c. Dominican Republic
4.	Shohei Ohtani	______	d. Australia
5.	Mariana Rivera	______	e. Puerto Rico
6.	Minnie Minoso	______	f. The Netherlands
7.	Fernando Valenzuela	______	g. Venezuela
8.	David Ortiz	______	h. Germany
9.	Max Kepler	______	i. Panama
10.	Liam Hendriks	______	j. Cuba

21. LEVEL: MULTIPLE

TROUBLE IN PAIRS . . . It's two puzzles in one. First, unscramble the letters on each line to spell an English word (Ex: EGVI unscrambled would be GIVE). Next, on the line <u>before</u> and <u>after</u> each unscrambled word, enter the first letter (on the left) and last letter (on the right). Then, unscramble the letters on the lines (go down each column) to reveal the last names of two baseball players. (Ex: For <u>G</u>IV<u>E</u> the G would be entered on the far left line; the E would be entered on the far right line; the G would be a letter contained in the <u>last</u> name of a MLB player; the E would be a letter contained in the <u>last</u> name of another player).

LEVEL: SINGLE

        N E O C   (Hint: Fairy tale beginning)

——   —— —— —— ——   ——

        I S A L   (Hint: Water craft part)

——   —— —— —— ——   ——

        O L T A   (Hint: Voice range)

——   —— —— —— ——   ——

        R C N A   (Hint: Illegal drugs agent)

——   —— —— —— ——   ——

Player's last name   Player's last name

________________   ________________

LEVEL: DOUBLE

        A S B D E   (Hint: Necklace part)

——   —— —— —— —— ——   ——

        A N J I N   (Hint: Warrior)

——   —— —— —— —— ——   ——

        A K K I H   (Hint: Pants)

——   —— —— —— —— ——   ——

U C S M R   (Hint: Seen in rugby)

—— —— —— —— —— ——

R L A T A   (Hint: Site of "I do")

—— —— —— —— —— ——

Player's last name   Player's last name

————————   ————————

LEVEL: TRIPLE

B E L O B G   (Hint: Eat greedily)

—— —— —— —— —— ——   ——

N R I O I G   (Hint: Beginning or cause)

—— —— —— —— —— ——   ——

L P N A A M   (Hint: Used in bombs)

—— —— —— —— —— ——   ——

T P C S I R   (Hint: Something written)

—— —— —— —— —— ——   ——

U I A G N A   (Hint: Lizard)

—— —— —— —— —— ——   ——

L B R E R A   (Hint: Vessel; keg)

—— —— —— —— —— ——   ——

Player's last name   Player's last name

————————   ————————

L B E A U N R   (Hint: Cloud)

___ ___ ___ ___ ___ ___ ___

B R B R A U H   (Hint: Garden crop)

___ ___ ___ ___ ___ ___ ___

O L P N O M A (Hint: Satire)

___ ___ ___ ___ ___ ___ ___

O I E H R E C   (Hint: Farewell)

___ ___ ___ ___ ___ ___ ___

I S N G H A U   (Hint: Distress)

___ ___ ___ ___ ___ ___ ___

R T T I H Y F   (Hint: Frugality)

___ ___ ___ ___ ___ ___ ___

Player's last name   Player's last name

________________   ________________

22. LEVEL: SINGLE

WORD FIND - MLB CITIES . . . Every National League (NL) MLB city listed can be found in the grid of letters. (Note: Cities are listed below the grid).

Cities can be found in a straight line either horizontally, vertically, or diagonally. They may be read backward or forward. Cities can share letters as they cross over each other. Circle or underline the cities when you find them.

MLB CITIES - NATIONAL LEAGUE

```
C  S  P  W  O  H  U  F  W  R  C  A  U  S  W  A
A  I  I  I  I  G  G  I  M  A  I  M  A  Z  T  A
P  U  N  T  T  D  E  M  R  H  T  N  G  N  U  J
R  O  A  C  W  T  L  I  P  A  F  E  A  U  B  D
B  L  R  O  I  R  S  L  D  R  C  L  L  X  C  O
L  T  H  F  Q  N  E  B  A  N  T  J  Y  V  D  I
Q  N  R  A  R  D  N  N  U  A  A  L  C  M  N  L
Z  I  V  A  A  E  C  A  R  R  A  S  X  N  O  K
E  A  L  L  A  I  E  E  T  U  G  O  H  S  T  R
Z  S  I  C  S  N  B  K  E  I  E  H  A  O  G  O
C  H  I  C  A  G  O  D  U  L  C  N  S  D  N  Y
P  H  O  E  N  I  X  E  G  A  G  G  I  L  I  W
B  U  Q  D  Z  A  T  N  V  E  W  I  D  A  H  E
J  I  J  K  C  Y  Q  V  L  N  C  L  G  T  S  N
W  Q  W  U  C  X  H  E  R  G  U  L  I  P  A  P
R  E  J  N  P  I  S  R  U  G  J  O  I  M  W  G
```

ATLANTA	CHICAGO	CINCINNATI
DENVER	LOSANGELES	MIAMI
MILWAUKEE	NEWYORK	PHILADELPHIA
PHOENIX	PITTSBURGH	SANFRANCISCO
SANDIEGO	SAINTLOUIS	WASHINGTONDC

23. LEVEL: DOUBLE

TEAM MASCOTS . . . Most MLB teams have a mascot which usually is a big crowd-pleaser at games. Some teams have multiple mascots (which often are used at different events such as games, publicity events, advertising, etc.). The goal of this puzzler is to match the team (1–10 below in the left column) with the mascot in the right column (a–j).[4]

TEAM	(a-j)	Mascot
1. Pirates	__	a. TC Bear
2. Padres	__	b. Phanatic
3. Brewers	__	c. Swinging Friar
4. Twins	__	d. Parrot
5. Cardinals	__	e. Sluggerrr
6. Tigers	__	f. Orbit
7. Phillies	__	g. Bernie
8. Royals	__	h. Paws
9. White Sox	__	i. Fredbird
10. Astros	__	j. Southpaw

24. LEVEL: DOUBLE

FILL IN THE BLANKS . . . Fill in the blanks to reveal the names of players and a manager associated with a particular team. Every occurrence of every letter of that team's name has been filled in. Also, can you name the MLB team?

1. _ r e _ _ a _ _ _ _ _
2. _ _ e _ _ r r e
3. B _ b b _ _ _ _
4. R a b b _ _ _ a r a _ v _ _ _ e
5. _ a _ _ A a r _ _
6. _ r e _ _ _ e _ r e e _ a _
7. A _ _ r _ _ _ _ _ e s
8. _ _ _ _ _ e r _ _ _ e s
9. _ _ _ _ e A _ _ _ e s
10. _ a _ e _ _ r _ _ _

Team: ___________________________

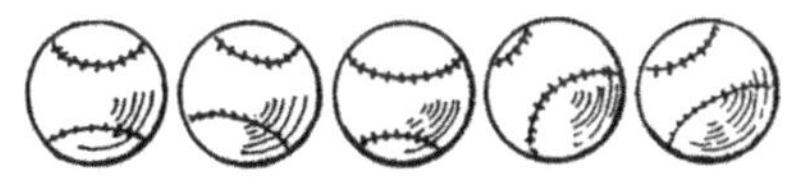

25. LEVEL: DOUBLE

TED, JOE, WILLIE, AND HANK . . . Ted Williams, Joe DiMaggio, Willie Mays, and Hank Aaron are four very famous MLB players. Each of them accomplished feats on the field that were the envy of their peers/contemporaries. Below are 10 trivia questions on Williams, DiMaggio, Mays, and Aaron. Correctly answer at least eight of the questions and land on second base with a stand-up **DOUBLE**. (Note: All answers follow the format – A, B, C, or D)

A. Ted Williams
B. Joe DiMaggio
C. Willie Mays
D. Hank Aaron

1. Which player had a 56-game hitting streak? ____ (A, B, C, or D)

2. Which player batted .406 for an entire season? ____

3. Which player never won a World Series championship? ____

4. Which player hit 700+ home runs? ____

5. Which player was a center fielder for a National League team? ____

6. Which player was a right fielder? ____

7. Which player batted left-handed? ____

8. Which player had the Polo Grounds as his "home field?" ____

9. Which player was known for his disagreements with the Press? ____

10. Which player was named League Most Valuable Player the most times? ____

26. LEVEL: MULTIPLE

BANANAGRAMS . . . I enjoy the Bananagrams game. If you're not familiar with the game, 144 plastic "tiles" with a letter on one side (A – Z) are laid face-down on a flat surface (a table for ex.), and 21 tiles are selected at random. (Each tile is about one-inch square.) Basically, (and to simplify the explanation) English words are formed from the 21 tiles.

For this puzzler, 21 letters are provided, and your job is to use any of the letters to form last names of past and current MLB players. Once a name is formed, ALL letters are used again to form a second name (and so forth). Here are the 21 letters and two examples.

A A E E I I S S T T R R O U N G L D B Y M

Two examples: BERRA (Yogi) can be formed from the "B," an "E," both "R" letters, and an "A." Replacing <u>all</u> letters so the original 21 can be used again, the name of STAUB (Rusty) can be formed. Note: The names of BELL and Boggs, for example, cannot be formed since only one "L" and one "G," respectively, are provided. How many names (any number of letters) can you list in three minutes?

Including the two examples:

$$3 - 5 \text{ names} = \textbf{SINGLE}$$
$$6 - 9 \text{ names} = \textbf{DOUBLE}$$
$$10 \text{ or } 11 \text{ names} = \textbf{TRIPLE}$$
$$12 \text{ or more} = \textbf{HOME RUN}$$

BERRA   STAUB   ________

________   ________   ________

________   ________   ________

________   ________   ________

________   ________   ________

27. LEVEL: SINGLE

VICTOR'S VOWELS . . . Victor is a sportswriter, but he has been a frustration to his editor due to his terrible spelling. In particular, Victor has an aversion to the five vowels of a, e, i, o, and u. Every story Victor writes contains no vowels. Can you help his editor by inserting the vowels on the blank lines in the beginning sentences of the following story Victor filed? Words are separated with a slash to make reading easier.

P_rf_ct/ w_ _th_r/ f_r/ b_s_b_ll/ gr_ _t_d/ th_/ n_ _rly/ 40,000/ d_ _-h_rd/ f_ns/ y_st_rd_y./ Th_/ g_m_/ "f_r_w_rks"/ st_rt_d/ q_ _ckly/ _n/ th_/ _p_n_ng/ fr_m_/ w_th/ _/ gr_nd/ sl_m/ t_/ _n_rg_z_/ th_/ cr_wd./

28. LEVEL: SINGLE

WORD FIND - MURDERERS' ROW . . . The late 1920s New York Yankees, especially the 1927 team, were known as Murderers' Row. They dominated teams while winning 110 games (154-game schedule), won the American League (AL) pennant by 19 games, and swept the Pirates in the World Series, 4 games to none.

Consider this: During the regular season the Yankees were first in the AL in Runs, Hits, HRs, Triples, Total Bases, Batting Average (.316 without pitchers), Base on Balls, On-Base-Percentage, Slugging Percentage, and more! In addition to these numbers, the "Pinstripes" also had the pitching in 1927 to complement the great offensive output. Yankees' pitchers (in AL) were first in Wins, Earned Run Average (ERA), Shut-Outs Thrown, Least Hits Allowed, Least Runs Allowed, and the list goes on.

The Word Find below contains 12 members of the 1927 Yankees team – Murderers' Row. Find all 12 names and scamper to first base with a **SINGLE**.

1927 NEW YORK YANKEES – MURDERERS' ROW

```
Y  S  B  M  O  C  M  P  P  G
B  I  D  X  Z  O  E  P  U  I
D  U  G  A  N  L  U  E  N  R
A  L  N  N  E  L  S  N  T  H
F  Q  A  R  P  I  E  N  D  E
P  P  O  Z  P  N  L  O  K  G
T  O  G  T  Z  S  X  C  H  B
M  Y  G  I  N  E  O  K  T  L
S  H  O  C  K  E  R  C  U  U
Y  V  L  H  O  Q  U  I  R  A
```

COLLINS	COMBS	DUGAN	GEHRIG
HOYT	KOENIG	LAZZERI	MEUSEL
MOORE	PENNOCK	RUTH	SHOCKER

29. LEVEL: DOUBLE

COMPOUND WORDS . . . Many MLB players have last names that are common English words like Jimmy <u>KEY</u> and Ricky <u>STONE</u>. A compound word can be made by merging KEY and STONE (<u>keystone</u>). Below are last names of MLB players. Make compound words from last names based on the clues. For example, the first answer (clue=compass direction) is <u>northeast</u> ("north" from first column and "east" (second column). First column always comes first.

Ball	Bird	1. <u>northeast</u> (Compass direction)
Winter	Wood	2. ________________ (Door fastener repairman)
Grace	Day	3. ________________ (Small, avian creature)
Lock	Green	4________________ (Radio/phone distress call)
Rose	**East**	5. ________________ (MLB games played here)
Blue	Smith	6. ________________ (Elvis Presley home)
North	Park	7. ________________ (Medicinal/flavor aromatic)
May	Land	8. ________________ (Tropical tree)

30. LEVEL: DOUBLE

STRIKE THREE . . . Some words just seem to go together. If one is speaking about baseball, STRIKE THREE and THREE OUTS, fit the bill.

If one of the words is "given" like STRIKE, and the complete answer is two words or syllables, STRIKE _____ could become STRIKE THREE. If the THREE becomes the first word of the following answer, then THREE ______ could become THREE OUTS. For example, STRIKE ________ (an umpire shouts this) or _______ OUTS (defensive team strives for this)

This becomes:

STRIKE <u>THREE</u>
<u>THREE</u> OUTS

Now it's your turn. Complete the puzzle (clues provided) and pull into second base with a **DOUBLE**.

<u>Clue</u>[5] (Not all clues or answers relate to baseball)

1. Home _______		**4-Bagger**
2. _______ Down		**Caught between Bases**
3. _______ _______		**Direction of a gale or breeze; leeward**
4. _______ Up		**Pitching motion**
5. _______ _______		**Batter on-deck (waiting to hit)**
6. _______ Year		**To win the following season**

31. LEVEL: MULTIPLE

BASEBALL SCORES AND MUSIC SCORES[6] . . . Baseball and Music have been "connected" for a long, long time. Even before the 1908 song *Take Me Out to the Ballgame* was popular, the post Civil War-era gave fans of the game <u>and</u> the more-established polka crowd, the successful *Base Ball Polka*.

Throughout the years of MLB, numerous song-writers have woven "Baseball" into their lyrics. For some of the songs, the National Pastime has been the main focus, while others have used baseball as an analogy for life off the field.

Here are six baseball tunes. Can you match the song with the recording artist/lyricist who made the musical composition famous? <u>Put the number of the song next to the artist/lyricist</u>. Get all six questions correct and earn a **HOME RUN**, five correct is good for a **TRIPLE**, four correct is a **DOUBLE**, and three correct is worth a **SINGLE**. Don't despair if you get two or less correct – you were in the on-deck circle when the inning ended!

SONG		**ARTIST/LYRICIST**
1. *Centerfield*	____	The Treniers
2. *The Cheap Seats*	____	Kenny Rogers
3. *There Used to be a Ballpark*	____	Bruce Springsteen
4. *Say Hey (The Willie Mays Song)*	____	Frank Sinatra
5. *Glory Days*	____	Alabama
6. *The Greatest*	____	John Fogerty

EARLY INNINGS ANSWERS

1.

    1. me   4. me

    2. peanuts   5. they

    3. never   6. old

2.

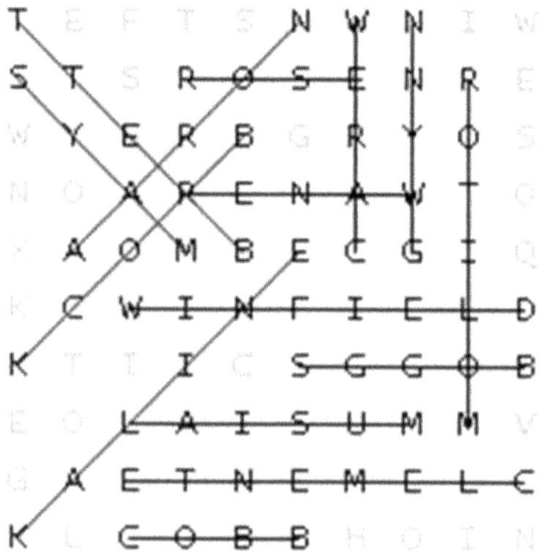

AARON	BOGGS	BRETT
BROCK	CAREW	CLEMENTE
COBB	GWYNN	KALINE
MAYS	MOLITOR	MUSIAL
ROSE	WANER	WINFIELD

3.

1. Hurt (also Thru)   4. Return
2. Diners (also Rinsed)   5. Grease (also Agrees)
3. Tutor

(Note: All words/anagrams from the
sixth edition, 2018 Scrabble US Dictionary)

4.

1. Barry Bonds
2. Hank Aaron
3. Babe Ruth
4. Alex Rodriguez
5. Albert Pujols
(Note: Through the 2022 season)

5.

Here are a few Joes. There are many others.

Mauer, Morgan, Jimenez, Gallo, Ryan, Lucchesi, Cronin, Niekro, Torre, Carter, Pepitone, Adcock, Kelley, Giradi, Jay, Wendle, Medwick, McGinnity, Christopher, Dugan, Pignatano, etc.

6.

A. Argument   F. Fly Ball
B. Baseball   G. Grounder
C. Coach   H. Hot Dog
D. Dugout   I. Infield
E. Error   J. Jacket   (All are sample answers.)

7.

1. Pete Rose
2. Hank Aaron
3. Nolan Ryan
4. Bob Feller
5. Willie Mays

6. Cy Young
7. St. Louis Cardinals
8. Cooperstown, New York
9. Babe Ruth
10. Ty Cobb

8.

Baseball Stadium Theme – BA are the two letters that begin the word tower. (These answers are only a sample. Yours may be different).

1. BAT
2. BALL
3. BASES
4. BATTER
5. BATTING
6. BASEPATH
7. BASELINES
8. BAREHANDED
9. BASERUNNING
10. BACKPEDALLED (some dictionaries use only one "L" in back-pedalled, while other dictionaries hyphenate the word).

9.

(Answers can have different first names)

1.	. . . **jet er**red . . .	Derek **Jeter**
2.	. . . o**ver land er**ratically . . .	Justin **Verlander**
3.	. . . Cre**w" hit e**ight . . .	Bill **White**
4.	. . . doc**tor re**viewed . . .	Joe **Torre**
5.	. . . cari**bou to n**ewts . . .	Jim **Bouton**
6.	. . . gram**mar is** . . .	Roger **Maris**
7.	. . . cilan**tro, ut**ilizing . . .	Mike **Trout**
8.	. . . deni**al on so**ftware . . .	Pete **Alonso**
9.	. . . Afghani**stan "ton**gue" . . .	Giancarlo **Stanton**
10.	. . . bron**co le**apt . . .	Gerrit **Cole**

10.

Here are just a few correct answers.

1.	Water (bottle)	6.	Ice
2.	Rosin	7.	Seeds (sunflower)
3.	Trainer	8.	Tape
4.	Bench	9.	Yankees
5.	Astros	10.	Towel

11.

Harmon Killebrew hit 573 MLB home runs.

12.

(The underlined letter has been changed at each step. There are other correct answers.)

B U N T
B U N <u>K</u>
B U <u>L</u> K
B <u>A</u> L K
<u>W</u> A L K

13.

Here are just a few 3-letter last names: Jimmy **KEY**, Mel **OTT**, Carlos **MAY**, Nellie **FOX**, Billy **COX**, Steve **SAX**, Jon **JAY**, Vernon **LAW**, Charlie **LAU**, Bill **LEE**, Jason **BAY**, Preacher **ROE**, Jermaine **DYE**, Byung-Hyun **KIM**, Dummy **HOY**, Jayson **NIX**, Jace **FRY**, Dillon **GEE**, Gavin **LUX**, Tommy **Mee**, Darin **RUF**, Griffin **JAX**, and many more.

14.

1. Small wall
2. Low throw
3. Cub flub
4. Chilly Willie
5. Brew Crew
6. Joe's toes
7. Blue's shoes

15.

1. <u>Jerry</u> was the winner with a BA of <u>.343</u>.
   (175 base hits/510 at-bats = .343)
2. Attendance = <u>40,001</u>; [(40,007) − (9) + (3)] = 40,001];
   Note: Square root of 81 is 9, (i.e., 9 x 9 = 81).

16.

1. double	6. leap
2. lead	7. bobble
3. clean up	8. left-hander
4. left fielder	9. cycle
5. handle	10. stole

17.

1.	. . . a cri**b**, **a t**able . . .	bat
2.	. . . windo**w I n**ever . . .	win
3.	. . . dep**th, row**ing . . .	throw
4.	. . . Men**sa' ve**rified . . .	save
5.	. . . atti**c at Ch**urch . . .	catch
6.	. . . Dimi**tri ple**aded . . .	triple

18.

The following are a few one-syllable baseball terms. There are many more:

Bat, ball, safe, out, catch, throw, pitch, strike, walk, balk, slide, lead, base, hit, run, fly, block, tag, line, coach, home, mound, box, hop, steal, run

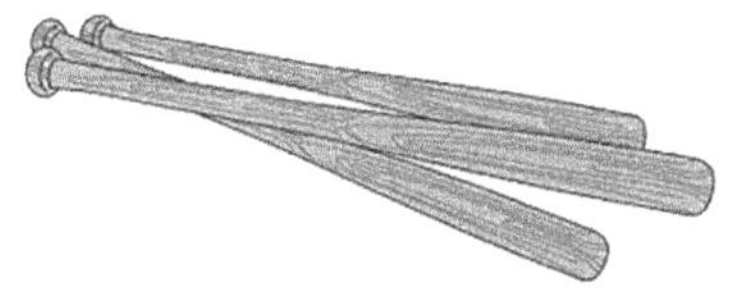

19.

2016 WORLD SERIES CHAMPION CHICAGO CUBS

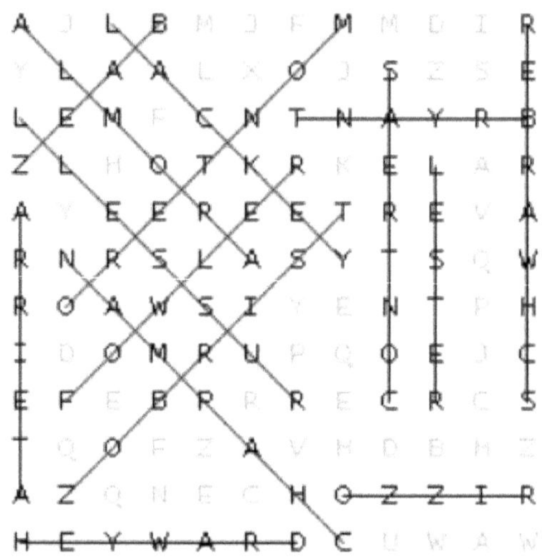

ALMORA	ARRIETA	BAEZ	BRYANT	CHAPMAN
CONTREAS	FOWLER	HEYWARD	LACKEY	LESTER
MONTERO	RIZZO	RUSSELL	SCHWARBER	ZOBRIST

20.

1.	e	6.	j
2.	g	7.	b
3.	f	8.	c
4.	a	9.	h
5.	i	10.	d

21.

LEVEL: SINGLE

O̲NCE̲, S̲AIL̲, A̲LTO̲, N̲ARC̲.
The players are S̲ano̲ and C̲ole̲.

LEVEL: DOUBLE

B̲EADS̲, N̲INJA̲, K̲HAKI̲, S̲CRUM̲, A̲LTAR̲.
The players are B̲anks̲ and M̲aris̲.

LEVEL: TRIPLE

G̲OBBLE̲, O̲RIGIN̲, N̲APALM̲, S̲CRIPT̲, I̲GUANA̲, B̲ARREL̲.
The players are G̲IBSO̲N and M̲ANTL̲E.

LEVEL: HOME RUN

N̲EBULAR̲, R̲HUBARB̲, L̲AMPOON̲, C̲HEERIO̲, A̲NGUISH̲, T̲HRIFTY̲.
The players are C̲ARLTO̲N and H̲ORNSB̲Y.

22.

MLB CITIES—NATIONAL LEAGUE

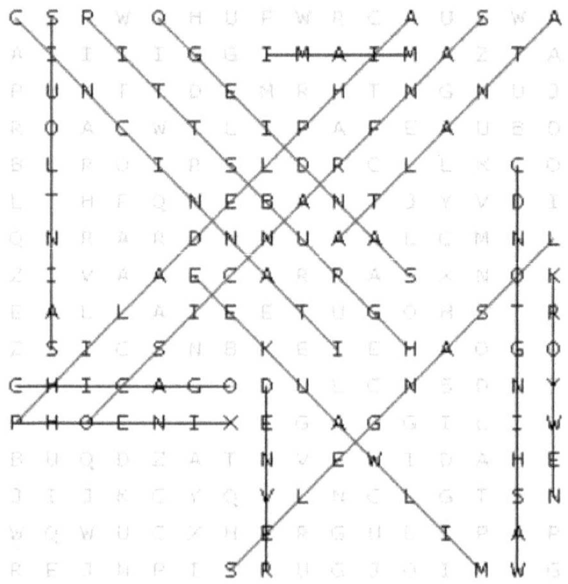

ATLANTA	CHICAGO	CINCINNATI
DENVER	LOSANGELES	MIAMI
MILWAUKEE	NEWYORK	PHILADELPHIA
PHOENIX	PITTSBURGH	SANFRANCISCO
SANDIEGO	SAINTLOUIS	WASHINGTONDC

23.

1.	d	6.	h
2.	c	7.	b
3.	g	8.	e
4.	a	9.	j
5.	i	10.	f

24.

1. Greg Maddux	6. Freddie Freeman
2. Joe Torre	7. Andruw Jones
3. Bobby Cox	8. Chipper Jones
4. Rabbit Maranville	9. Ozzie Albies
5. Hank Aaron	10. Dale Murphy

Team: Braves (Boston, Milwaukee, Atlanta)

25.

1.   B (1941)
2.   A (1941)
3.   A
4.   D (755 career home runs)
5.   C
6.   D
7.   A
8.   C
9.   A
10.   B (1939, 1941, 1947)

26.

Here are a few names that can be made with the 21 letters. There are many more.

Berra	Staub	Rose	Riley	Trout	Lee	Betts	Sales
Sano	Torre	Martin	Albies	Maris	Groat	Milton	Lester
Stone	Lau	Alou	Alomar	Mays	Maye	Brett	Tolan
Doerr	Doby	Mota	Dean	Gibson			

27.

Perfect weather for baseball greeted the nearly 40,000 die-hard fans yesterday. The game "fireworks" started quickly in the opening frame with a grand slam to energize the crowd.

28.

1927 NEW YORK YANKEES – MURDERERS' ROW

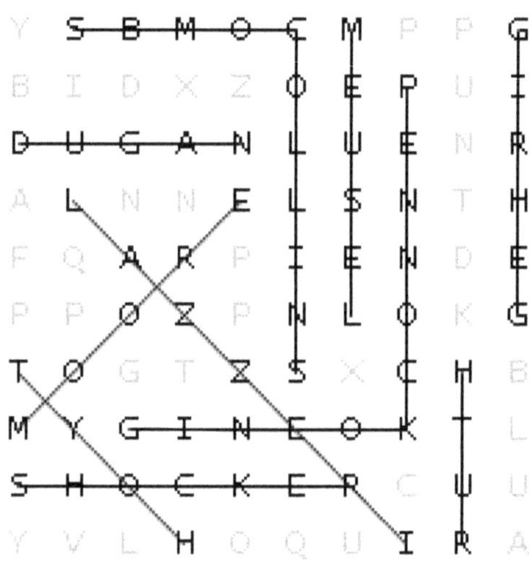

COLLINS	COMBS	DUGAN	GEHRIG
HOYT	KOENIG	LAZZERI	MEUSEL
MOORE	PENNOCK	RUTH	SHOCKER

29.

1. Northeast
2. Locksmith
3. Bluebird
4. Mayday
5. Ballpark
6. Graceland
7. Wintergreen
8. Rosewood

30.

1.   Home Run
2.   Run Down (rundown)
3.   Down Wind (downwind)
4.   Wind Up (windup)
5.   Up Next
6.   Next Year

31.

1. John Fogerty   4. The Treniers
2. Alabama   5. Bruce Springsteen
3. Frank Sinatra   6. Kenny Rogers

[1]https://loc.gov/item/ihas.200153239/ (accessed February 23, 2023).

[2]https://loc.gov/item/ihas.200153239/ (accessed February 23, 2023).

[3]There was also a Jim Adduci that played between 1983 and 1989.

[4]https://www.mlb.com/all-star/play-ball-park/mascots (accessed May 24, 2022).

[5](https://www.Merriam-Webster.com (compound words per Merriam-Webster online dictionary; accessed July 31, 2022).

[6]Memories and Dreams, Volume 44, Number 2, The National Baseball Hall of Fame: Cooperstown, NY. "Pop Goes the Baseball," pp. 32-33. Mark Preston.

[7]https://word.tips/unscramble (accessed March 30, 2021).

2

MIDDLE INNINGS

1. LEVEL: DOUBLE

INFIELD SLANG . . . Second base is known as the "keystone sack." This is just one of many terms or baseball "slang" that is heard in the infield of MLB and all the way down to Little League play. Here is some additional infield slang.[1] How many can you correctly identify?

SLANG	ANSWER
Around the Horn	________________
Baltimore Chop	________________
Candy Hop	________________
Cue Ball	________________
The Dish	________________
Hot Corner	________________
Neighborhood Play	________________
Stone Hands	________________

2. LEVEL: SINGLE

ONE LETTER AT A TIME . . . Pete Rose is the all-time MLB hits leader with 4,256. Quite an achievement! Can you go from the <u>Rose</u> to <u>Hits</u> by changing only one letter and forming a common English word at each step (three words are required). You can't change the order of the letters.

ROSE

_________   (repetition of learning something)

_________   (decay or decompose – [plural])

_________   (rise in temperature – [plural])

HITS

3. LEVEL: MULTIPLE

BANANAGRAMS . . . I enjoy the Bananagrams game. If you're not familiar with the game, 144 plastic "tiles" with a letter on one side (A – Z) are laid face-down on a flat surface, and 21 tiles are selected at random. Basically, (and to simplify the explanation) English words are formed from the 21 tiles.

For this puzzler, 21 letters are provided, and your job is to use any of the letters to form words (English!) of three (3) or more letters. Once a word is formed, all letters can be used again to form a second word (and so forth). Here are the 21 letters and two examples to better explain the process.

The letters are: A EE II O B DD C FF G H K NN P RR T

Two examples: DEER can be formed from the "D," both the "E" letters, and the "R." Replacing <u>all</u> letters so the original 21 can be used again, the word CENT can be formed. Note: The words CABBAGE and BITTER, for example, cannot be formed since only one "A" and one "B" (for CABBAGE), and one "T" (for BITTER), are provided. Proper nouns (like Akron, India, or Berra) are not allowed.

How many words (non-proper nouns) of <u>three or more letters</u> can you list in <u>three (3) minutes</u>?

Including the two examples:

10 – 14 words = **SINGLE**

15 – 19 words = **DOUBLE**

20 – 24 words = **TRIPLE**

25 or more = **HOME RUN**

<u>DEER</u>   <u>CENT</u>   ________   ________

________   ________   ________   ________

________   ________   ________   ________

________   ________   ________   ________

________   ________   ________   ________

________   ________   ________   ________

________   ________   ________   ________

4. LEVEL: DOUBLE

WHICH TEAM IS IT? . . . Many teams have nicknames that are known by most die-hard baseball fans. Other teams had groups of players that in a particular year, or years, were known by a special name. And still other teams had a rallying cry or moniker for a specific year.

Your job is to put the letter found by the team name in the blank by the corresponding nickname, slogan, or phrase. Eight (8) or more correct earns you a stand-up **DOUBLE.** Note: #1 is given to you.

1. The Pinstripes	_c_	a. New York Mets
2. Gas House Gang	___	b. Philadelphia Phillies
3. Pale Hose	___	c. New York Yankees
4. Big ___ Machine	___	d. St. Louis Cardinals
5. Beat 'Em Bucs	___	e. Milwaukee Brewers
6. The Northsiders	___	f. Chicago White Sox
7. The Brew Crew	___	g. Cincinnati Reds
8. Miracle ___	___	h. Chicago Cubs
9. Whiz Kids	___	i. Brooklyn Dodgers
10. Boys of Summer	___	j. Pittsburgh Pirates

5. LEVEL: DOUBLE

X, Y, Z . . . The last three letters of the alphabet. Letters you undoubtedly learned at a very early age! All the answers in this puzzler contain either an X, Y, or Z, and these letters are provided prior to the question. The answer can be one or two+ words but the letters (X, Y, Z) need only be in <u>one</u> of the words. Also, X or Y or Z can be a single or double letter.

X   1.   Playing beyond nine (9) innings.   ______________________

Y   2.   Team name (such as Cubs or Twins) ______________________

X   3.   Designated spot for 3rd base coach. ______________________

Y   4.   Third base runner scores on a batted ball caught by the center fielder <u>before</u> the ball touches the ground.

                                      ____

Z   5.   Batter bunts ball to score runner. ______________________

X   6.   City where the Diamondbacks play. ______________________

Z   7.   Served at some concession stands. ______________________

Y   8.   2 putouts often involving shortstop, 2nd baseman, and 1st baseman. ______________________

Z   9.   Weather that doesn't stop play. ______________________

Y   10. Team knots score with this tally. ______________________

6. LEVEL: SINGLE

WORD FIND - SAVES . . . Back in the day (prior to 1969!) "saves" by a pitcher were not officially recorded by MLB. Starting in the 1969 season, the "save" rule was adopted (and amended for the 1974 and 1975 seasons). Incidentally, baseball researchers have worked through the official statistics retro actively to calculate saves for all major league seasons prior to 1969.[2]

The following Word Find contains 15 of the all-time MLB save leaders (often called "stoppers" or "closers") at the end of the 2022 season. Player names are listed under the puzzler. Can you find all of them?

DIRECTIONS:
Find the name in the puzzle. *Words can go in any direction. Words can share letters as they cross over each other.*

```
N  V  W  J  F  I  N  G  E  R  S  N
A  C  C  N  A  R  R  C  L  E  L  O
T  N  J  J  I  N  K  Y  M  N  E  D
H  I  W  V  H  E  S  I  Q  G  R  R
A  C  E  T  R  I  O  E  F  A  B  A
N  R  I  S  H  Z  S  C  N  W  M  E
A  M  L  U  P  O  Q  R  N  Z  I  R
S  E  J  D  M  L  V  U  E  A  K  W
Y  Q  N  A  M  F  F  O  H  Y  R  F
H  Z  T  L  O  M  S  I  I  A  E  F
P  A  P  E  L  B  O  N  J  L  B  M
Z  E  U  G  I  R  D  O  R  H  C  V
```

ECKERSLEY	FINGERS	FRANCO	HOFFMAN
JANSEN	KIMBREL	MEYERS	NATHAN
PAPELBON	REARDON	RIVERA	RODRIGUEZ
SMITH	SMOLTZ	WAGNER	

7. LEVEL: MULTIPLE

LET'S PLAY TWO . . . The trademark phrase of the Cubs' Ernie Banks—Let's Play Two—is known by baseball fans, regardless of team affiliation. But many facts about "Mr. Cub" are less well-known.

The following four questions about this Hall of Fame member will test your knowledge of Ernie Banks.

One correct: **SINGLE**, Two correct: **DOUBLE**,
Three correct: **TRIPLE**, Four Correct: **HOME RUN**

1. What state was Ernie Banks born in?

    a. Florida   c. Alabama
    b. Illinois   d. Texas

2. In 1954, Banks appeared in 154 games. Since he only appeared in 10 games in 1953, the year 1954 was considered Banks' rookie year. Was Banks selected as 1954 Rookie-of-the-Year?

    a. yes   b. no

3. Was Ernie Banks elected to the Hall of Fame in his first year of eligibility?

    a. yes   b. no

4. Ernie Banks hit 512 career home runs. What are the most HRs Banks hit in one season?

a. 54

c. 40

b. 47

d. 58

8. LEVEL: TRIPLE

HIDDEN NAMES . . . This puzzle involves finding a last name of a MLB player that is hidden somewhere in the sentence. The correct answer could be spread over one, two, or several words. All punctuation, capital letters, etc., should be ignored when searching for the hidden name. For example, the sentence: [All entered but few departed] contains the last name of the Philadelphia Phillies' first black superstar, and one of MLB's most feared hitters in the 1960s, Dick Allen. Do you see it? [All entered but few departed].

Can you find the hidden MLB player's name (last name) in the following sentences? Hint: All players are retired.

1. The car slid on an ice-covered road into the snowbank, slightly damaging the side mirror. ___________ (Clue: Wrigley Field)

2. The boys flocked around the carnival's magician while the girls preferred "Guru Theodore," the fortune teller. ___________ (Clue: Outstanding HR hitter for Yankees)

3. The girl and boy erased the board after school. _______________ (Clue: St. Louis 3RD Baseman who starred in the 1960's)

4. The bill was inside another one of Tim's books. ___________
   (Clue: Gas House Gang pitcher)

5. When the plate broke in Mary Jane's sink, I nervously picked
   up the pieces. _________ (Former HR hitter and Mets
   broadcaster)

6. The most obnoxious child in the class was Rueben Dermott.
   ___________ (Clue: Chief)

7. The wedding reception was fairly calm until the band played
   a polka, line dance, and the 'chicken' song in succession.
   ___________ (Clue: Former Detroit Tigers outfielder)

8. At the costume party, Diane shouted at the host while
   sipping her cognac, "I'm Olive Oil, Popeye's honey!"
   ___________ (Clue: "Super sub" on the 1960 World
   Champion Pirates)

9. The injury report included the trio of Marc, Roberto, and
   Fernando, bystanders in the wrong place at the wrong time.
   ___________ (Clue: Broke AL color barrier in 1947)

10. "Carry and hike and paddle" was a slogan Mike adopted
    after five days of portages. _______________ (Strikeout king)

9. LEVEL: DOUBLE

MIENTKIEWICZ . . . I named this puzzler after the last name of a former
Minnesota Twins player (1998 – 2009) – Doug Mientkiewicz
(Mientkiewicz played for a total of seven teams in his MLB career). Many
common English words can be made from the letters in M I E N T K I E W
I C Z such as ten, wet, time, etc. Notice (as an example) that there is only
one "t" in Mientkiewicz so the word "ten" can be made but not "tent."
Also, after making the word "ten," all letters are returned to the name
Mientkiewicz, and then the word "wet" can be made.

Your job is to take a player name (which I provide) and make words that are synonyms (have the same, or nearly the same, meaning) of underlined word(s) in a sentence or phrase. M I E N T K I E W I C Z will serve as an illustration.

The sample sentence is: The home team <u>victory</u> (3 letters) was witnessed by a <u>father and his brother</u> (3 letters), and the father's <u>15 year-old son</u> (4 letters).

The <u>underlined word(s)</u> (in the sentence above) can be replaced with a word formed from the letters in M I E N T K I E W I C Z. The number of letters in the replacement word are in (parenthesis).

The answer to the above sentence is: The home team WIN was witnessed by the MEN, and the father's TEEN. Notice that the words "WIN," "MEN," and "TEEN" can all be formed from the letters in M I E N T K I E W I C Z with replacement of all letters after each word is made.

This puzzler uses the name G A R D E N H I R E. (Before Ron Gardenhire managed the Twins and Tigers, he was an infielder with the Mets.)

Your task is to form a word from the letters in G A R D E N H I R E that replaces the underlined words in the following sentence:

On a <u>challenge</u> (4 letters) from friends, Johnny <u>secretly placed</u> (3 letters) the tickets in the glove box of his <u>18-wheeler</u> (3 letters).

    1. challenge   _____   2. secretly placed   _____

    3. 18-wheeler _____

10. LEVEL: HOME RUN

WORD TOWER . . . Every word in a word tower begins with the same two letters. You build the tower by increasing the length of each word by one letter. For instance, a word tower on the letters FA could include: FAn, FAir, FAult, etc.

Let's see how far you can go on a "baseball theme" (i.e., all words must be something one could find/related to/describing a baseball game held in a MLB stadium). (*Note: Proper nouns are not allowed, and you can't just add an s to the <u>next</u> word in your tower. For example, if your three-letter word is "hit," your four-letter word <u>cannot</u> be "hits." You can only use "hits" if the word directly proceeding it was NOT "hit.")* For a big (**HOME RUN**) challenge, get to "tower-level 10" in three minutes.

<u>Baseball Theme – first two letters are FL</u> (also, the hint (in parentheses), refers to the <u>word listed</u> in the Answers Section, although the word you <u>select</u> can be entirely different since there can be more than one correct answer).

1. FL___ (noun: ball hit in air)

2. FL___ ___ (verb: HR hitters can taunt pitchers this way.)

3. FL___ ___ ___

    (noun: often seen at or near the top of stadiums)

4. FL___ ___ ___ ___

    (verb: batters facing curve ball pitchers often do this)

5. FL___ ___ ___ ___ ___

    (verb: coach at 3rd base does this to stop runners)

6. FL___ ___ ___ ___ ___ ___

(adjective: a pitch obviously thrown at a batter)

7. FL___ ___ ___ ___ ___ ___ ___

(noun: support for objects that "wave" in the breeze)

8. FL___ ___ ___ ___ ___ ___ ___

(adjective: some players described this way)

9. FL___ ___ ___ ___ ___ ___ ___ ___

(noun: bending easily without breaking; pliability)

10. FL___ ___ ___ ___ ___ ___ ___ ___ ___

(noun: hard throwing pitcher)

11. LEVEL: DOUBLE

U, V, W . . . All the answers in this puzzler <u>begin </u>with either a **U, V,** or **W**. The answer can be one or two+ words but the letters (U, V, W) need only be the first letter in <u>one</u> of the words. Get all 10 correct answers and you can enjoy the stadium view from second base (**DOUBLE)**.

1. Arbiter _________________

2. A win _________________

3. A fan needs this some days _________________

4. Pitcher losing control of strike zone _________________

5. Leads you to your stadium seat ___ _____________

6. Winner of this MLB event has bragging rights all winter

____

7. Not recorded as an "at-bat" in determining Batting Average

   ____

8. When baseball executives get-together in the off-season

   ____

9. Sells you ballpark souvenirs _______________

10. A seat near top of stadium _______________

12. LEVEL: DOUBLE

ANAGRAMS . . . The letters of the MLB player's <u>last</u> name in this list can be rearranged in multiple ways to form other words. I provide the name; your job is to come up with <u>one</u> or <u>two</u> anagrams (as indicated by the blank spaces) of <u>all</u> the letters in the given (last) name of the player. For example: The letters in the last name of Jorge "SOLER" can be rearranged to spell the two words: "loser" and "roles (or "sorel").

Solve these seven questions/anagrams in four minutes and you can rest while standing on second base with a **DOUBLE**.

1. Nolan RYAN   _______________

2. Willie MAYS   _______________

3. Tony OLIVA   _______________

4. Tom SEAVER   _______________

5. Frank BAKER   _______________

6. Mickey MANTLE   _______________ _______________

7. Johnny EVERS   _______________ _______________

13. LEVEL: TRIPLE

STATEWIDE TRIVIA . . . This puzzler is a test on (1) your knowledge of the 50 states that comprise the United States of America, and (2) unscrambling letters to reveal the name of a great baseball player.

Your task is to use the <u>first</u> letter of each answer (state) and unscramble the letters to form the player's name. Note: The blank lines (___) indicate the number of letters in each state. For example, if an answer was TEXAS, then there would be five blank lines—one line for each letter in TEXAS. The first letter (<u>T</u>) would be one of eight letters to unscramble.

	STATE	NICKNAME OR HINT
1.	___ ___ ___ ___ ___ ___ ___	Peach State
2.	___ ___ ___ ___ ___ ___ ___ ___ ___	Mayo Clinic
3.	___ ___ ___ ___ ___ ___ ___ ___	Sooner State
4.	___ ___ ___ ___ ___ ___ ___ ___	First State
5.	___ ___ ___ ___ ___ ___ ___ ___	Land of Lincoln
6.	___ ___ ___ ___ ___ ___ ___	Masters' golf home
7.	___ ___ ___ ___ ___ ___	Large State
8.	___ ___ ___ ___ ___	Potato State

Player's Name ____

(unscrambling and using all eight letters)

14. LEVEL: DOUBLE

VICTOR'S VOWELS . . . Victor is a sportswriter but he has an aversion to the five vowels of a, e, i, o, and u. Victor drives his editor "nuts" due to his terrible spelling. Can you help his editor by inserting the five vowels into the first two sentences of this story Victor filed? Missing vowels in each word is/are indicated by the numbers in parenthesis ().

Th(1) hm(2) tm(2) scrd(2) rly(2) nd(1) ftn(2) n(1) rtng(3) th(1) vstrs(3) 10 t(1) n(2), wth(1) fr(2) rns(1) n(1) th(1) frst(1) nnng(2), tw(1) n(1) th(1) scnd(2), nd(1) tw(1) mr(2) n(1) th(1) thrd(1). Th(1) gm(2) ws(1) smngly(3) vr(2) by th(1) frth(2) nnng(2).

15. LEVEL: SINGLE

WORD FIND - HALL OF FAME PITCHERS . . . Baseball Hall of Fame (HOF) inductees are an elite group of people. (Notice I didn't say ". . . group of <u>men</u> . . . " as one woman, Effa Manley, was inducted in 2006).[3] Nearly 350 players, managers, umpires, and executives are currently enshrined in Cooperstown.

Pitchers are three times more likely to be inducted into the Baseball Hall of Fame than other position players. At the MLB level, a team might have a baker's dozen of pitchers, but only two or three catchers.[4]

In the "word find" below are the names of 21 pitchers – all in the Baseball HOF. If your favorite HOF hurler is not on the list of 21, don't be discouraged. There are over 80 of them![5]

Instructions:

Player names can go in any direction.

Player names can share letters as they cross over each other.

Circle, underline, or mark the player names.

HALL OF FAME PITCHERS

```
N  W  A  D  D  E  L  L  Q  N  R  G
O  A  U  P  E  G  W  W  H  J  R  A
T  N  H  A  P  S  D  A  Y  E  E  R
T  O  O  S  I  R  R  O  M  N  T  E
U  S  S  T  B  B  Y  U  I  K  N  V
S  B  R  S  L  R  S  J  E  I  U  I
D  I  E  E  Y  R  D  A  V  N  H  R
D  G  G  A  L  T  A  A  K  S  D  E
W  G  N  V  E  L  L  C  U  R  G  T
N  B  I  E  V  G  E  Q  O  V  R  T
K  G  F  R  E  G  V  F  W  Z  Q  U
X  B  U  N  N  I  N  G  P  C  F  S
```

BLYLEVEN	FORD	CARLTON
DRYSDALE	FELLER	FINGERS
BUNNING	GIBSON	GLAVINE
HUNTER	JENKINS	KAAT
MORRIS	RIVERA	RYAN
SEAVER	SPAHN	SUTTER
SUTTON	WADDELL	WYNN

WHERE DO YOU HAIL FROM, STRANGER? . . . MLB players, current and past, come from every state in the U. S. including territories/possessions, countries north, south, east, and west of MLB stadiums, and various nations around the globe. How many of the following players can you match with their place of <u>birth</u>? (Remember, it's the <u>birthplace</u> of the players we're matching, not where they were raised, retired, off-season home, etc.). Four players correctly matched is worth a **SINGLE**, five or six correct answers earns you a **DOUBLE**, seven or eight correct qualifies for a **TRIPLE**, and nine or ten correct is worth a **HOME RUN**.

(a -j)

1. Babe Ruth	______	a. California
2. Sammy Sosa	______	b. Virginia
3. Mookie Betts	______	c. New Jersey
4. Maury Wills	______	d. Dominican Republic
5. Justin Verlander	______	e. Texas
6. Alex Bregman	______	f. Washington, D. C.
7. Joe DiMaggio	______	g. Maryland
8. Derek Jeter	______	h. Puerto Rico
9. Roberto Clemente	______	i. Tennessee
10. Ernie Banks	______	j. New Mexico

WHAT'S THE CONNECTION? . . . Given nine MLB player names randomly placed in a grid, can you find the three groups of names that are connected AND explain why they are connected? Here's a sample grid:

Mickey Mantle	Chipper Jones	Eddie Mathews
Juan Marichal	Derek Jeter	Willie Mays
Willie McCovey	Hank Aaron	Lou Gehrig

GROUP 1 NAMES:	THEME:
Mantle, Jeter, Gehrig	Yankees

GROUP 2 NAMES:	THEME
Jones, Mathews, Aaron	Braves

GROUP 3 NAMES:	THEME
Marichal, Mays, McCovey	Giants

Here is a grid of MLB teams for you to ponder. Get the names and the themes correct, and "Going, Going, Gone." Your towering blast cleared the center field fence for a **HOME RUN**.

Phillies	Reds	Marlins
Mariners	Padres	Royals
Pirates	Rangers	Mets

<u>GROUP 1 NAMES:</u>   <u>THEME</u>

__________________________   __________________

<u>GROUP 2 NAMES:</u>   <u>THEME</u>

__________________________   __________________

<u>GROUP 3 NAMES:</u>   <u>THEME</u>

__________________________   __________________

18. LEVEL: DOUBLE

COMPOUND WORDS . . . Many MLB players have last names that are common English words like Wally <u>Moon</u> (1954 – 1965) and T.J. <u>Beam</u> (2006 – 2008). A compound word is formed by combining Moon and Beam (<u>moonbeam</u>). Below are 16 last names (in two columns) of former or current MLB players (eight questions). Make compound words from the last names based on the clues. For example, the first answer (clue: artificial illumination) is <u>floodlight</u>. (Numbers three and five are plural.)

Brown   Fisher   1. <u>floodlight</u>   (Artificial illumination)

White   Ward   2. _______________   (Very large island)

<u>Flood</u>   Sand   3. _______________   (Common in Minnesota [pl.])

Cotton	Light	4.	______________	(Bird found near water)
Green	Banks	5.	______________	(Auto tires, pl.)
Quick	Ball	6.	______________	(Tree; sometimes called Poplar)
Lee	Land	7.	______________	(Game similar to squash)
Snow	Walls	8.	______________	(Avoid when walking)
King	Stone	9.	______________	(Downwind; away from the wind)
Hand	Wood	10.	______________	(New York City townhouse)

19. LEVEL: DOUBLE

ER . . . This puzzler requires an answer with the letters "E" and "R" in <u>consecutive</u> order in a word. Answers can be at the start, end, or somewhere "inside" the word. All answers <u>can be seen</u> at a MLB game.

1. A misplay or miscue. ______________

2. Person that keeps players healthy. ______________

3. Answer to #2 often uses a type of this treatment.

    ____

4. What the 1st, 2nd, and 3rd baseman plus shortstop are called.

    ____

5. Player that throws the ball from the mound must put his/her foot on this. ______________

6. Position #2 if you're keeping score. ______________

7. Players in question 4 (above) field many of these over an entire season. ______________

8. The name of a ball hit squarely (often called a "rope").

____

9. The name of a ball hit softly in the air, and often falls

between two or more players. _______________

10. Another name for the pitcher. _______________

20. LEVEL: DOUBLE

OPS . . . On-Base Plus Slugging (OPS) is one of many new sabermetric statistics to be used as a measure of productivity for baseball players. According to MLB, OPS adds on-base percentage and slugging percentage to get one number that unites the two. It's meant to combine how well a hitter can reach base, with how well he can hit for average and power. It can also be used in evaluating pitchers; when used in this context, it is referred to as "OPS against."[6]

I'm not going to ask you OPS-type questions for this puzzler. However, I am going to provide a series of questions/statements where all answers begin with either an "O," a "P," or a "S." Note: The blank lines indicate the number of words in a typical answer. Only <u>one</u> of the words/answer must begin with an "O," a "P," or a "S."

1. One "away" in a half-inning. _____________ _____________

2. Umpire cry (shout) at beginning of a game. ___________

____

3. To "swipe" a base. ___________

4. Where runs, hits, etc., are posted. _____________

5. A fast runner. _____________

6. The position player (1 – 9) typically not known as a HR threat.

   ____

7. Music comes from this. _____________

8. Dark and cloudy day for baseball. _____________

9. Batters are happy when this number is high. _______ _______

10. Fans often do this before and during game. _____________

21. LEVEL: MULTIPLE

THE BLACK HOUSE . . . Many MLB players have last names that are common words. For example, the sentence, "The black house has a gray roof" looks ordinary <u>except</u> the last names of four MLB players are embedded in it: Bud **Black** (1981-1995), Tom **House** (1971-1978), Sonny **Gray** (active in 2022), and Phil **Roof** (1961-1977). (Note: There are additional MLB players named Black, House, Gray, and Roof; the names selected are only examples.)

For this puzzler, the following paragraph has 21 last names of MLB players (past and present). Ignoring capitalization and punctuation, can you find all 21 names/words? For a **SINGLE**, find at least 10 names, 11 to 14 names is a **DOUBLE**, 15 to 19 names is a **TRIPLE**, and if you can find 20 or 21 names you've earned a long **HOME RUN**!

"I rose rapidly when the ring from the alarm clock woke me from a deep sleep. It was still dark as confirmed by a peek out my window. My goal for the day was to take a long walk in the quiet woods. I hurriedly dressed in blue jeans, did a fast brush of my teeth, splashed my face at the sink, and made sure to grab some cash for a much-deserved donut after my hike. I gulped down some yogurt, stuffed granola bars into my pants pockets, and stepped into my new brown winter boots. I ambled through the front door while the church bell chimed. And then I saw the new layer of white snow. "Good," I said to myself, "The weather's on my side for seeing animal tracks today."

22. LEVEL: TRIPLE

THE AVERAGE IS . . . Many baseball aficionados associate a particular batting average (BA) with a particular player; or a batting average with a "standard" of some type.

Match the left column (numbers 1-10) with the correct/associated BA (alpha's a–j). Get 8 or more correct, and you just hit a **TRIPLE**.

1. Ted Williams' 1941 BA		a. .300
2. Mendoza "line"		b. .250
3. Cobb's lifetime BA		c. .000
4. Who'll hit this again in MLB?		d. .400
5. George Brett's 1980 BA		e. .256

6. Benchmark BA for many MLB players   f. .328

7. BA if 4 hits & 12 outs are made   g. .406

8. BA (?) if 71 yr. old author played MLB   h. .366

9. Harmon Killebrew's lifetime BA   i. .200

10. In 2021 Trea Turner's MLB leading BA   j. .390

___ ___ ___ ___ ___ ___ ___ ___ ___ ___
1.   2.   3.   4.   5.   6.   7.   8.   9.   10.

23. LEVEL: MULTIPLE

CAMPY . . . This was the nickname for Roy Campanella. Campy had a long career in the Negro Leagues (1937 – 1945) as well as with the Brooklyn Dodgers (1948 – 1957) in the NL. With Brooklyn, he was an eight-time All-Star, Most Valuable Player (MVP) three times, and a World Series champion in 1955. He was inducted into the Hall of Fame in 1969.

In addition to being a great baseball player, Roy Campanella had an "above average" number of letters in his last name. The name "Campanella," with 10 letters, is excellent for this next puzzler.

How many <u>three or more letter words</u> can you form from the letters in CAMPANELLA in three minutes? (with <u>replacement</u> of <u>all</u> letters after each word is formed)

Up to 14 words: **SINGLE**

15 – 17: **DOUBLE**

18 – 20: **TRIPLE**

21 or more: **HOME RUN**

An example, the word "men" can be formed from the last name. Replacing all letters so 10 letters still remain, the word "man" can be formed.

Again, the 10 letters: C A M P A N E L L A

men   man   ________   ________   ________

________   ________   ________   ________   ________

________   ________   ________   ________   ________

________   ________   ________   ________   ________

________   ________   ________   ________   ________

________   ________   ________   ________   ________

24. LEVEL: DOUBLE

ONE LETTER AT A TIME . . . Barry Bonds hit 73 home runs in 2001 eclipsing Mark McGwire's total of 70 homers from 1998. Although controversy swirls around Bonds' (and McGwires') achievements, MLB recognizes the numbers on their official website.[7]

Can you go from the <u>Bonds </u>to <u>Homer</u> by changing only one letter at a time (five total letters) and forming a common English word at each step (three words are required). You can't change the order of the letters.

B O N D S (Note: All hints have plural answers)

1.________ (Hint: Skeleton has these)

2.________ (Hint: To sharpen)

3.________ (Hint: A town has these)

H O M E R

25. LEVEL: TRIPLE

CROSSWORD . . . Crosswords are quite popular today. Some folks, in fact, contend that doing crosswords on a regular basis are linked to a sharper brain in later life.[8] Others note, that yes, crosswords are fun for people of all ages, and that crosswords are a good brain exercise, but stop short of making long-term predictions.[9] Obviously, more research is needed on the long-term value of doing crossword puzzles.

Regardless of the side of the fence you land on regarding crosswords, one is offered here as your next puzzler. The crossword below is baseball-related (it better be, you're probably thinking, since this is a baseball book!). Can you complete it? If so, you can proudly say, "I hit a **TRIPLE.**"

Find the word in the puzzle.
Words can go across or down.
Words can share letters when they cross over each other.

BASEBALL CROSSWORD

ACROSS

1. MEMBER OF ORIGINAL HALL OF FAME CLASS
3. 2021 AL MVP
4. CAREER MLB LEADER IN "GAMES PLAYED"
5. WEARS THE "TOOLS OF IGNORANCE"
7. MEMBER OF "300 WIN CLUB"
11. 2022 MINNESOTA TWINS MANAGER
14. ANOTHER NAME FOR PITCHERS MOUND
15. TINKER TO EVERS TO ___________
18. CAREER MLB LEADER IN "HITS BY A RIGHT-HANDED BATTER"
19. "SINGLE-SEASON" MLB LEADER IN "HITS"
20. ILLEGAL PITCH

DOWN

1. FLASHES "SIGNS" TO BATTER AND BASE RUNNER(S)
2. SKIPPER
4. MOST AL TEAM WINS IN 2022
6. CAREER MLB LEADER IN "RUNS SCORED"
8. PERSON CALLED "BLUE"
9. CAREER MLB LEADER IN "STRIKEOUTS BY A BATTER"
10. CLOSER (POSITION)
12. ANOTHER NAME FOR A BASEBALL BAT
13. MOST NL TEAM WINS IN 2021
16. PLAYING FIELD ENCLOSURE
17. MEMBER OF ORIGINAL HALL OF FAME CLASS

26. LEVEL: TRIPLE

ANAGRAMS . . . The letters of each MLB player's <u>last</u> name in this list can be rearranged in multiple ways to form other words. I provide the name; your job is to come up with an anagram of <u>all</u> the letters in the family (last) name of the player. For example, two anagrams of HUDSON (Tim) are HOUNDS and UNSHOD.

1. Rollie FINGERS   _______________

2. Bob LEMON   _______________

3. Mickey COCHRANE   _______________

4. Pete ALONSO   _______________

5. Dave STEWART   _______________

6. Harrison BADER   _______________

7. Chili DAVIS   _______________(pl.)

27. LEVEL: DOUBLE

ONE LETTER AT A TIME . . . Go from the top word to the bottom word by changing only one letter and forming a common English word at each step. You can't change the order of the letters.

If you're successful in going from BASE to DIRT, you can scamper into second base with a **DOUBLE**.

B A S E

______

_______ (Hint: Challenge)

______

D I R T

28. LEVEL: MULTIPLE

WHAT'S IN A NAME? . . . The last name or surname "Johnson" is one of the most common names in the country. As you might expect, "Johnson" is a very common last name in MLB as well.

To test your knowledge of MLB players, past and present, how many with the last name of "Johnson" can you name in <u>3 minutes</u>? To get you started, here are two Hall of Famers with the last name of "Johnson" – Walter and Randy. Including the two players just given, if you name 5-9 you hit a **SINGLE**, 10-15 a **DOUBLE**, 16-20 a **TRIPLE**, and 21 or more deserves **HOME RUN** status. (Note: First name must be unique to a player; for example, there have been three different MLB players named Randy Johnson, BUT only <u>one</u> Randy Johnson can be listed in this puzzler.)

Walter, Randy, ____

____

____

____

____

29. LEVEL: MULTIPLE

VALENZUELA AND VAUGHAN . . . Victor Vanucci is a very strange fellow. Victor has many strange habits or quirks. One of these is his obsession with the letter "V," including MLB players whose last name begins with a "V." Specifically, Fernando Valenzuela (1980 – 1997) and Arky Vaughan (1932 – 1948) are two of his favorites, along with (and more recently), Justin Verlander (active in 2022) and Shane Victorino (2003 – 2015).

How many MLB players, past and present, can you name in 3 minutes whose last name begins with a "V?" You can include the four named above to give you a running start.

If you name:

   6 players or less in 3 minutes, round first base with a **SINGLE**;

   7 – 8 players, you just hit a **DOUBLE**;

   9 – 12 players, and slide into third in a cloud of dust with a **TRIPLE**;

   and 13 or more players, you've earned a **HOME RUN**.

Valenzuela, Vaughan, Verlander, Victorino,______________________________

____

____

____

____

30. LEVEL: DOUBLE

STRIKE THREE . . . Some words just seem to go together, like STRIKE THREE and THREE OUTS, if one is speaking about baseball.

If one of the words is "given" like STRIKE, and the complete answer is two words or syllables, STRIKE _____ could become STRIKE THREE. If the THREE becomes the first word of the following answer, then THREE _______ could become THREE OUTS. For example,

      STRIKE ________ (batter never wants to hear umpire shout this)

      _______ OUTS (defensive team always striving for this)

becomes:

      STRIKE THREE

      THREE OUTS

Now it's your turn. Complete the puzzle (clues given) and pull into second with a **DOUBLE**.

Clues[10]

(Not all clues or answers relate to baseball)

1. <u>Pitch</u> ______   Pitcher's game limit

2. ______ ______   Rocket ship blast off

3. <u>Down</u> ______   A name for a HR

4. ______ <u>Ball</u>   Name for "Baseball" at local level

5. ______ ______   "National Pastime" contest

6. ______ <u>Time</u>   When first pitch is thrown

7. _____ _____ Player or umpire delay in action

8. _____ _____ Where three of nine players are found

9. _____ <u>Level</u> Usually good seats at baseball stadium

31. LEVEL: DOUBLE

HOMONYMS . . . Homonyms (that include homophones and homographs[11]) are words that sound the same (same pronunciation) but are spelled differently and have different meanings. An "everyday" example is *see* (meaning vision) and *sea* (body of water). A baseball example is *threw* (The shortstop *threw* the ball) and *through* (The ball missed the cut-off and went *through* to the plate).

Below are 10 sentences where the blanks in the sentences indicate a homonym is missing. Can you determine the correct spelling and meanings of the missing words/homonyms?

1. The home team __________ the game by __________ run.

2. The __________ of the new ballpark was on old swamp land but had fan-friendly __________ lines.

3. The damp morning __________ on the field meant Grapefruit League rookies had to __________ their drills in the afternoon.

4. The __________ or price of the stadium hot dogs did not seem __________ to the father of three children.

5. The runner __________ around the bases despite missing the week-
   end doubleheader with chills and stomach pain caused by the
   __________ .

6. The __________ men in the box seats let out a loud __________
   when the home team failed to score.

7. The __________ player on the team __________ all the signs and
   bench signals without having to be reminded.

8. The long home run shattered a window __________ but did not
   cause any "__________ and suffering" to the occupants.

9. One __________ of the 9th place hitter is to __________ over the
   batting order.

10. The lineup's number __________ batter blistered a "__________
    hot__________ handle" walk-off single.

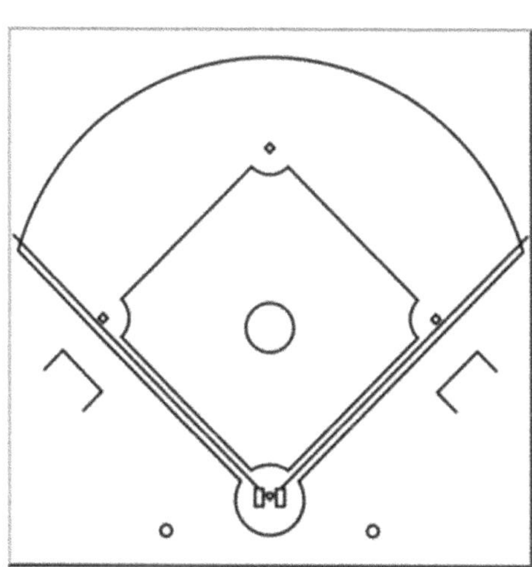

BASEBALL SLANG . . . Baseball has a unique language that is all its own. Below are eight baseball terms or "slang" words/phrases that have developed over the years. How many can you identify? Note: There are more answers (a − l) than questions (1 − 8).

<table>
<tr><td>1. Battery</td><td>a. Umpire</td></tr>
<tr><td>2. Can of corn</td><td>b. Relief pitcher</td></tr>
<tr><td>3. The Box</td><td>c. Line drive</td></tr>
<tr><td>4. The Show</td><td>d. Fly ball easy to catch</td></tr>
<tr><td>5. Yard</td><td>e. Brief stay in Major Leagues</td></tr>
<tr><td>6. Southpaw</td><td>f. Bases clearing triple</td></tr>
<tr><td>7. Blue</td><td>g. Pitcher's mound</td></tr>
<tr><td>8. Cup of coffee</td><td>h. Righthanded pitcher</td></tr>
<tr><td></td><td>i. Lefthanded pitcher</td></tr>
<tr><td></td><td>j. Pitcher and catcher</td></tr>
<tr><td></td><td>k. Home Run</td></tr>
<tr><td></td><td>l. MLB</td></tr>
</table>

___ ___ ___ ___ ___ ___ ___ ___
1.   2.   3.   4.   5.   6.   7.   8.

MIDDLE INNINGS ANSWERS

1.

Your description of the correct answer may differ from the language below.

1. A play that goes third-to-second-to-first
2. A hit that bounces high in the air off the dirt in front of home plate
3. A ball hit with a nice, easy bounce right to a fielder
4. A ball hit off the end of the bat
5. Home plate
6. Third base
7. Usually the first part of a double play, when a fielder doesn't tag the base but gets the out call from the umpire
8. A bad fielder

2.

There may be more than one correct answer! Here's what I came up with.

ROSE
ROTE
ROTS
HOTS
HITS

3.

Here are a few words that can be made with the 21 letters.

DEER   CENT   BAT   CAT   FAT   HAT   PAT   GNAT
BOG   FOG   TON   BED   CON   HOG   KNOB   CRATE
COB   DIN   FIN   GIN   TRAP   DATE   PACK   TRACK
HATE   FROG   GAIN   RAIN   TRAIN   HIP   TAP   CRANE
DRIP   HIP   HID   KNIFE   FIGHT   GEEK   NEAT   TRAFFIC
FIND   HIDE   TOAD   GOAT   BOAT   ROTE   NOTE   POKE

4.

1. c   6. h
2. d   7. e
3. f   8. a
4. g   9. b
5. j   10. i

5.

Some of the following answers are examples only.

1.   Extra innings
2.   Royals, Yankees, Rays, or Blue Jays
3.   Coach's box or just box
4.   Sacrifice fly
5.   Squeeze (play) or Suicide/Safety squeeze
6.   Phoenix
7.   Pretzel(s)
8.   Double play
9.   Drizzle
10.   Tying run

6.

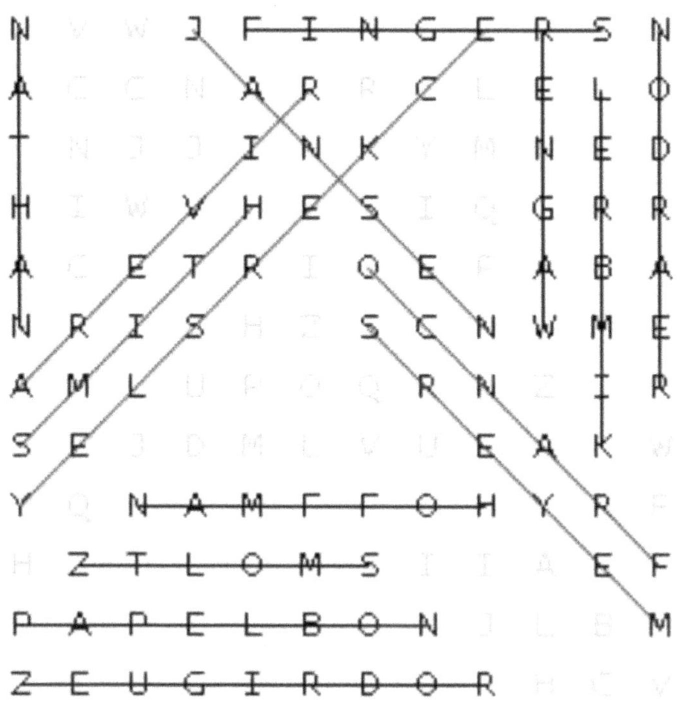

ECKERSLEY   FINGERS   FRANCO   HOFFMAN

JANSEN   KIMBREL   MEYERS   NATHAN

PAPELBON   REARDON   RIVERA   RODRIGUEZ

SMITH   SMOLTZ   WAGNER

7.

1. d   3. a

2. b   4. b

8.

1. . . . snow**bank, s**lightly . . .	Ernie **Banks**
2. . . . "Gu**ru Th**eodore," . . .	Babe **Ruth**
3. . . . **boy er**ased . . .	Ken **Boyer**
4. . . . insi**de an**other . . .	Dizzy **Dean**
5. . . . sin**k, I ner**vously . . .	Ralph **Kiner**
6. . . . Rue**ben Der**mott.	Chief **Bender**
7. . . . pol**ka, line** . . .	Al **Kaline**
8. . . . cogna**c, "I'm Oli**ve…	Gino **Cimoli**
9. . . . Fernan**do, by**standers . . .	Larry **Doby**
10. "Car**ry and** . . .	Nolan **Ryan**

9.

1. dare
2. hid
3. rig

10.

Word Tower answers can differ from one person to another.
Here are some possible answers.

1.	FLY	6.	FLAGRANT
2.	FLIP (Bat)	7.	FLAGPOLES
3.	FLAGS	8.	FLAMBOYANT
4.	FLINCH	9.	FLEXIBILITY
5.	FLAGGED	10.	FLAMETHROWER

11.

1.	**U**mpire	6.	**W**orld Series
2.	**V**ictory	7.	**W**alk
3.	**U**mbrella	8.	**W**inter Meetings
4.	**W**ild	9.	**V**endor
5.	**U**sher	10.	**U**pper Deck

12.

1.	yarn	5.	brake or break
2.	yams	6.	mental, lament, or mantel
3.	viola	7.	serve, sever, veers, or verse
4.	averse or reaves		

13.

1.	**G**eorgia	5.	**I**llinois
2.	**M**innesota	6.	**G**eorgia
3.	**O**klahoma	7.	**A**laska
4.	**D**elaware	8.	**I**daho

PLAYER NAME: **DiMaggio**

14.

Answers are underlined.

The h<u>o</u>me t<u>ea</u>m sc<u>o</u>r<u>e</u>d <u>ea</u>rly <u>a</u>nd <u>o</u>ft<u>e</u>n <u>i</u>n r<u>o</u>uti<u>n</u>g th<u>e</u> v<u>i</u>s<u>i</u>t<u>o</u>rs 10 t<u>o</u> <u>o</u>n<u>e</u>, w<u>i</u>th f<u>o</u>ur r<u>u</u>ns <u>i</u>n th<u>e</u> f<u>i</u>rst <u>i</u>nni<u>n</u>g, tw<u>o</u> <u>i</u>n th<u>e</u> s<u>e</u>c<u>o</u>nd, <u>a</u>nd tw<u>o</u> m<u>o</u>r<u>e</u> <u>i</u>n th<u>e</u> th<u>i</u>rd. Th<u>e</u> g<u>a</u>m<u>e</u> w<u>a</u>s s<u>ee</u>m<u>i</u>ngly <u>o</u>v<u>e</u>r by th<u>e</u> f<u>o</u>urth <u>i</u>nni<u>n</u>g.

15.

HALL OF FAME PITCHERS

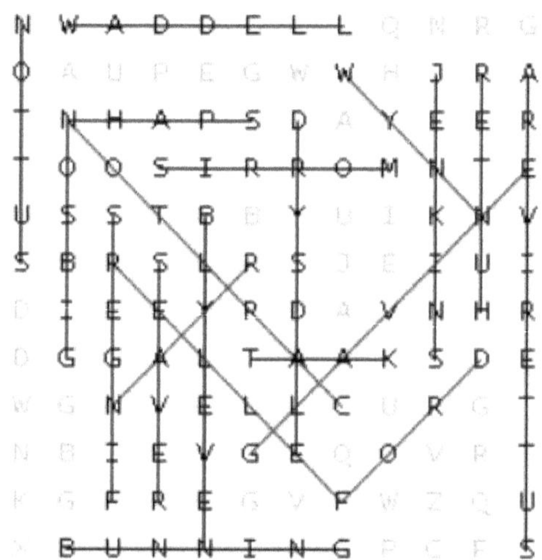

BLYLEVEN	FORD	CARLTON
DRYSDALE	FELLER	FINGERS
BUNNING	GIBSON	GLAVINE
HUNTER	JENKINS	KAAT
MORRIS	RIVERA	RYAN
SEAVER	SPAHN	SUTTER
SUTTON	WADDELL	WYNN

16.

1.	g	6.	j
2.	d	7.	a
3.	i	8.	c
4.	f	9.	h
5.	b	10.	e

17.

GROUP	THEME
1. Padres, Pirates, Phillies	All names begin with a "**P**"
2. Reds, Rangers, Royals	All names begin with a "**R**"
3. Mariners, Marlins, Mets	All names begin with an "**M**"

One solution provided; your answer may differ.

18.

1.	Floodlight	6.	Cottonwood
2.	Greenland	7.	Handball
3.	Snowbanks	8.	Quicksand
4.	Kingfisher	9.	Leeward
5.	Whitewalls	10.	Brownstone

19.

1.	Error	6.	Catcher
2.	Trainer	7.	Grounders
3.	Therapy	8.	Liner
4.	Infielders	9.	Blooper or Texas Leaguer
5.	Rubber	10.	Hurler

20.

1.	**O**ne Out	6.	**P**itcher
2.	**P**lay Ball	7.	**O**rgan
3.	**S**teal	8.	**O**vercast
4.	**S**coreboard	9.	**P**late Appearance
5.	**S**wift	10.	**S**ing

21.

The underlined words below are MLB player names. Let me know if I missed any!

"I <u>rose</u> rapidly when the <u>ring</u> from the alarm clock woke me from a deep sleep. It was still <u>dark</u> as confirmed by a <u>peek</u> out my window. My goal for the <u>day</u> was to take a <u>long</u> <u>walk</u> in the quiet <u>woods</u>. I hurriedly dressed in <u>blue</u> jeans, did a <u>fast</u> <u>brush</u> of my teeth, splashed my <u>face</u> at the sink, and made sure to grab some <u>cash</u> for a much-deserved donut after my hike. I gulped down some yogurt, stuffed granola bars into my pants pockets, and stepped into my new <u>brown</u> <u>winter</u> boots. I ambled through the front door while the <u>church</u> <u>bell</u> chimed. And then I saw the new layer of <u>white</u> <u>snow</u>. '<u>Good</u>," I said to myself, "The <u>weather's</u> on my side for seeing animal tracks today,"

Possible answers include: Pete **Rose** (1963-1986), Royce **Ring** (2005-2010), Al **Dark** (1946-1960), Steve **Peek** (1941), Zach **Day** (2002-2006), Dale **Long** (1951-1963), Bob **Walk** (1980-1993), Kerry **Wood** (1998-2012), Jake **Woods** (2005-2008), Vida **Blue** (1969-1986), Darcy **Fast** (1968), Bob **Brush** (1907), Roy **Face** (1953-1969), Kevin **Cash** (2002-2010), Trevor **Brown** (2015-2016), George **Winter** (1901-1908), Ryan **Church** (2004-2010), Josh **Bell** (active in 2022), Rick **White** (1994-2007), J.T. **Snow** (1992-2008), Andrew **Good** (2003-2005), and David **Weathers** (1991-2009).

22.

1.	g	6.	a
2.	i	7.	b
3.	h	8.	c
4.	d	9.	e
5.	j	10.	f

23.

There are many three+ letter words that can be formed from the letters in "CAMPANELLA." The following are a few of them:

Man, men, all, ape, elm, pan, pen, nap, lap, cap, map, ale, acne, amen, cell, came, name, lame, lean, lane, pane, mane, pale, male, peal, meal, mace, lace, pace, palm, plan, plea, camp, lamp, cape, camel, canal, clean, maple, lapel, lance, ample, pecan, alpaca, palace, almanac, panacea, and many more.

24.

There is more than one answer but here is a solution.

BONDS

BON<u>E</u>S

<u>H</u>ONES

HO<u>M</u>ES

HOMER

25.

26.

1. fringes
2. melon
3. encroach
4. saloon
5. swatter
6. beard or bread
7. divas

27.

There are multiple correct answers to this puzzler. One solution is given below. (The underlined letter was changed at each step).

B A S E

B A <u>R</u> E

<u>D</u> A R E

D <u>I</u> R E (or D A R <u>T</u>)

D I R T

28.

Here is a Johnson sampling of MLB.

Adam, Alan, Alex, Ben, Bill, Bob, Brian, Charles, Chris, Cliff, Dan, Davey, Deron, DJ, Earl, Elliot, Erik, Howard, Jerry, Jim, John Henry, Josh, Ken, Lance, Lou, Mark, Nick, Randy, Reed, Russ, Steve, Tyler, Vic, Wallace, Walter.

29.

The following is merely a sampling of MLB player names that begin with "V."

Valenzuela, Vaughan, Verlander, Victorino, Valdez, Vasquez, Ventura, Valaika, Valentine, Varitek, Vernon, VanMeter, Van Slyke, Vargas, Varsho, Velasquez, Vavra, Verdugo, Versalles, Villar, Valencia, Vincent, Virdon, Veale, Van Meter, Vance, Vander Meer and many more.

30.

1. Pitch Count	6. Game Time
2. Count Down	7. Time Out
3. Down Town (Downtown)	8. Out Field (Outfield)
4. Town Ball	9. Field Level
5. Ball Game	

31.

1. won; one	6. grown; groan
2. site; sight	7. new; knew
3. dew; do	8. pane; pain
4. fare; fair	9. role; roll
5. flew; flu	10. two; too; to

32.

1. j	5. k
2. d	6. i
3. g	7. a
4. l	8. e

[1]James Buckley Jr. *The National Baseball Hall of Fame Collection: Celebrating the Game's Greatest Players.* (Bellevue, WA: Epic Ink, 2020), 97.

[2]According to baseball-reference.com (accessed July 8, 2022), the rule on saves is as follows.

- A relief pitcher is awarded a **save** when he meets all three of the following conditions:
- He is the finishing pitcher in a game won by his club; and
- He is not the winning pitcher; and
- He qualifies under one of the following conditions:
    - ◊ He enters the game with a lead of no more than three runs and pitches for at least one inning; or
    - ◊ He enters the game, regardless of the score, with the potential tying run either on base, at bat, or on deck; or
    - ◊ He pitches for at least three innings. (The word "effectively" has been removed from the MLB rules.)
- No more than one save may be credited in each game. A pitcher who comes into the game in the circumstances described above is said to have a *save opportunity*.

[3]https://baseballhall.org/hall-of-famers/manley-effa (accessed July 20, 2022).

[4]John Veneziano, Ed. *National Baseball Hall of Fame and Museum: 2022 Yearbook.* (Lynn, MA: H.O. Zimman, Inc., 2022), 139-143.

[5]*Ibid.*

[6] https://www.mlb.com/glossary/standard-stats/on-base-plus-slugging (accessed July 26, 2022).

[7] https://www.mlb.com/stats/home-runs/all-time-totals (accessed July 28, 2022).

[8] https://blogs.scientificamerican.com/observations/this-is-your-brain-on-crosswords/ (accessed July 29, 2022).

[9] https://brainhq.com/brain-resources/cool-brain-facts-myths/brain-mythology/brain-myth-doing-crossword-puzzles-can-keep-your-brain-young/ (accessed July 29, 2022).

[10] (https://www.merriam-webster.com (compound words per Merriam-Webster online dictionary; accessed July 31, 2022).

[11] https://www.thoughtco.com and https://en.wikipedia.org/wiki/Homonym (accessed July 31, 2022).

3

LATE INNINGS

1. LEVEL: DOUBLE

BABE RUTH . . . Many MLB players, past and present, have a last name (Ruth, for example), that is a female's first name (Ruth, again). Mark Loretta (1995 – 2009), Steve Avery (1990 – 2003) and Austin Riley (active in 2022) are three other examples.

This puzzler requires matching MLB player's last name, which are female names, with the player's first name. The Babe Ruth example is #1. Note: To make the question a bit more challenging, there are more first names listed than are needed.

LAST NAME		FIRST NAME	
1. Ruth	_g_	a. Fred	k. Alan
2. Allison	____	b. Norm	l. Shorty
3. Reese	____	c. Marty	m. Mark
4. Rose	____	d. Bryce	n. Pee Wee
5. Lynn	____	e. Steve	
6. Grace	____	f. Trevor	
7. Harper	____	g. Babe	
8. Sherry	____	h. Bob	
9. Marion	____	i. Pete	
10. May	____	j. Henry	

2. LEVEL: SINGLE

WORD FIND - BATTING CHAMPS . . . To be a batting average champion in MLB is a feat that many players dream of, but few attain. The Word Find below contains names of some of the players (21) in the NL and AL that can claim "forever" that they lead their league in batting average for one year or more in the 20th or 21st Centuries. Note: The names include the first initial of the first name followed by the last name, i.e., Barry Bonds is listed as BBONDS.

Circle, underline, or mark in any way you choose the names of the batting champs in the grid. Find all 21 players and sprint to first with a SINGLE.

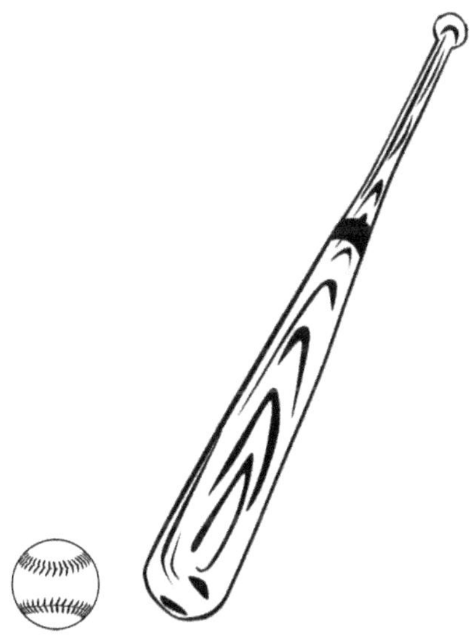

I O S E Q G J A L T U V E
K P T T U R N E R H J U J
U G T O Z E I I E C H E I
Z G E U S R E M Y I A I N
U J B N R J Y L D L M H K
S R M U E O U Z D E I A N
I E G C U R A H U Y L M G
E Y N N A L E H C C T E I
Q E G O M B N K M T O L D
M S F V J N R E L T N J N
D O S K H C O E K A X D H
N P Z E R I M A R M W J Z
B B O N D S J N X A T L W

Find the name in the puzzle.

Names can go in any direction.
Names can share letters as they cross over each other.

BBONDS	BPOSEY	CJONES	CYELICH
DJLEMAHIEU	DLEE	ISUZUKI	JALTUVE
JHAMILTON	JMAUER	JMORNEAU	JREYES
JSOTO	LWALKER	MBETTS	MCABRERA
MCUDDYER	MRAMIREZ	MYOUNG	TTURNER
YGURRIEL			

3. LEVEL: TRIPLE

FIRST NAMES—LAST NAMES . . . The <u>last</u> name of many MLB players is occasionally the <u>first</u> name of other people, sometimes famous "others." Below, a MLB player's first name (and clue) is provided. Your task is twofold: first, determine the player's <u>last</u> name which is also the <u>first</u> name of an "other," and then determine the last name of the "other" (actors/actresses or non-baseball athletes).

Make sure the player's <u>last</u> name corresponds to the <u>first</u> name of the "other." Example: <u>Tommy</u> <u>John</u> <u>Steinbeck</u>, for the "others" category of WRITERS. (Tommy John = Baseball player; John Steinbeck = Writer). I provided two answers to get you started. Solve this puzzler and end up on third base with a **TRIPLE**.

CATEGORY:
Actors/Actresses

CATEGORY:
Athletes (Non-Baseball)

1. <u>Nolan</u>   <u>Ryan</u>   <u>O'Neal</u>
   (HOF pitcher; retired
   as MLB strikeout leader)

   <u>Julio</u>   <u>Franco</u>   <u>Harris</u>
   (Rangers Batting Champ;
   final season at age 48)

2. <u>Joe</u> _______ _______
   (HOF second baseman
   & 2x MVP)

   <u>Carlos</u> _______ _______
   (Played 14 yrs. in MLB,
   1st team was White Sox)

3. <u>Josh</u> _______ _______
   (Began career (8 yrs.) with
   Pirates; multi-position player)

   <u>Fred</u> _______ _______
   (MVP & Batting Champ
   with Red Sox)

4. <u>Pee</u> <u>Wee</u> _______ _______   <u>Bill</u> _______ _______

   (HOF shortstop for Dodgers)   (HOF first baseman;

                                        batted .401 in 1930)

5. <u>Shane</u> _______ _______   <u>Dick</u> _______ _______

   (2x World Series Champ   (NL Rookie of Year in 1964;

   with Yankees)   MVP in 1972)

4. LEVEL: DOUBLE

A, B, C FOR THE HOF . . . The Baseball Hall of Fame (HOF) enshrines the greatest of the great. Members of the HOF include players, of course, and others who were associated with the game of baseball.[1] This puzzler tests your knowledge of AL and NL players from 1901 to 2022. Below are the first six letters of the alphabet. Your task is to list HOF players (one or two depending on the "blank" spaces provided), whose last name begins with one of the six letters. One name is provided to get you started.

A   1. <u>Aaron</u>

B   2. _________ _________

C   3. _________ _________

D   4. _________ _________

E   5. _________

("E" is limited because only two players in the 20th and 21st centuries are in the HOF. As a clue, one player is a pitcher and another a second baseman.)

F   6. _________

5. LEVEL: HOME RUN

BREAK THE CODE . . . Cryptograms are messages in substitution code. Break the code to read the message. For example, JOHNNY BENCH might become KPIOOZ CFODI if J is substituted for K, O for P, H for I, N for O, and so on. Can you break the code below? (Hint: Pay attention to the "order" of the "alphabet letters" when breaking the code. The JOHNNY BENCH example provides the "pattern.")

Uisff OM Bmm-Tubst jo 2019: Bouipoz

Sfoepo, Qfuf Bmpotp, boe Gsfeejf Gsffnbo.

_______ __ ___-_______ _ 2019: ________

_____, ___ ______, ___ _______ ________.

6. LEVEL: TRIPLE

CROSSWORD . . . Crosswords are quite popular today. Some folks, in fact, do crossword puzzles everyday since they are fun and challenging.

The crossword on the next page is baseball-related as all the clues and answers pertain to our National Pastime. Can you complete it? If so, you

can proudly say, "I hit a **TRIPLE**."

Use the clues to fill in the words below.

Words can go across or down.

Letters are shared when the words intersect.

ACROSS

2. FOUR BALLS
4. FIELD OF ____________
5. BASE
7. CALLED STRIKER LONG AGO
9. ANOTHER NAME FOR STRIKEOUT
10. PLAYER MISCUE
12. SINGLE SEASON MLB LEADER IN PLATE APPEARANCES
13. MEMBER OF ORIGINAL HALL OF FAME CLASS
15. DODGER BROADCASTER
16. DEFEAT
17. TEAM TRAINER USES A LOT OF THIS

DOWN

1. MEMBER OF "3,000 HIT CLUB"
3. MATERIAL OFTEN SPREAD ON GROUND AFTER A RAIN DELAY
4. ANOTHER NAME FOR HOME RUN
6. MEMBER OF ORIGINAL HALL OF FAME CLASS
8. MEMBER OF ORIGINAL HALL OF FAME CLASS
11. PLAYER'S NAME FOR A BLUE CLOUDLESS SKY
14. HIT IN BOTTOM OF 9TH THAT WINS GAME
15. HALL OF FAME THIRD BASEMAN

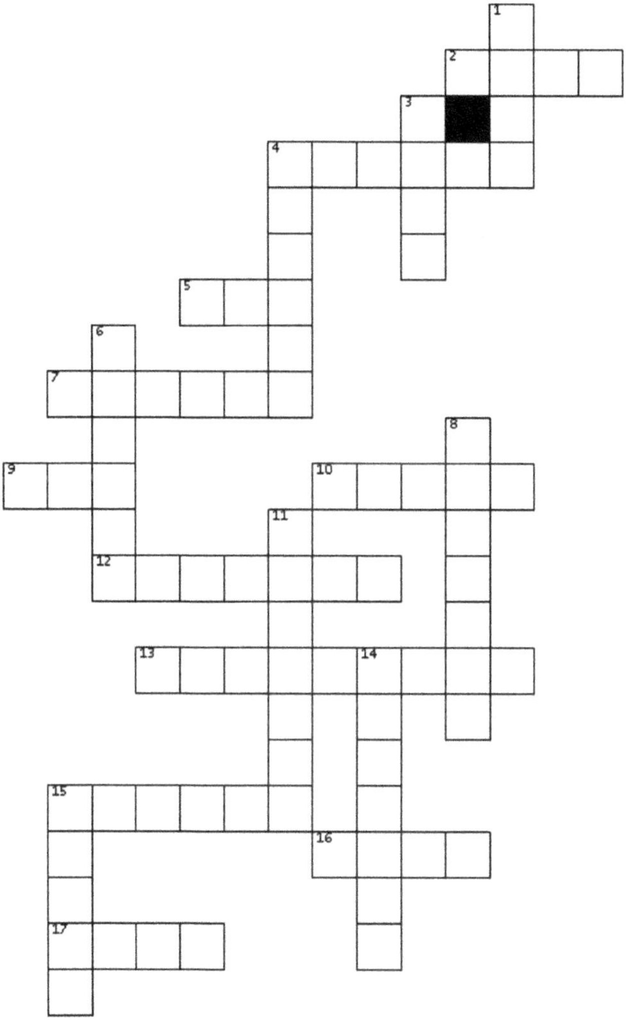
1
2
3
4
5
6
7
8
9
10
11
12
13
14
15
16
17

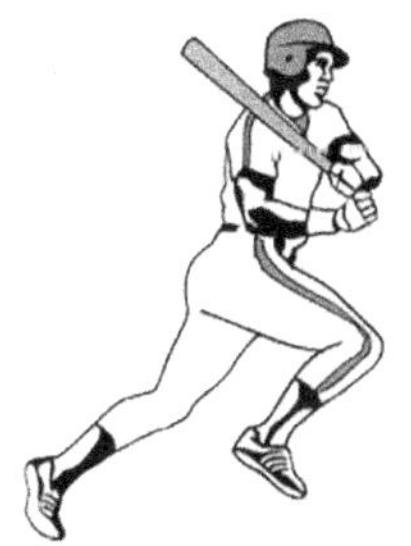

7. LEVEL: HOME RUN

NAME TOWER . . . Every name in a name tower begins with the same two letters. You build the tower by increasing the length of each name by one letter. For instance, a MLB name (last or surname) tower on the letters KE could include: KEY, KENT, KELLY, KEELER, KERSHAW, etc.

Let's see how far you can go on surnames of MLB player names (past and present) for the letters LA. To earn a **HOME RUN**, name 10 players in the word tower in <u>four minutes</u>.

MLB Player Names – first two letters are LA

1.　　LA_

2.　　LA_ _

3.　　LA_ _ _

4.　　LA_ _ _ _

5.　　LA_ _ _ _ _

6.　　LA_ _ _ _ _ _

7.　　LA_ _ _ _ _ _ _

8.　　LA_ _ _ _ _ _ _ _

9.　　LA_ _ _ _ _ _ _ _ _

10.　　LA_ _ _ _ _ _ _ _ _ _

Etc.

VICTOR'S VOWELS . . . Victor loves baseball but is a terrible speller. He has an aversion to vowels (a, e, i, o, u). When he writes a list of players, he always omits the vowels. Can you decipher this list of last names of players compiled by Victor? The blank spaces indicate the total number of letters in the name, and the player's primary position is given as (P) pitcher, (C) catcher, (IF) infielder, and (OF) outfielder. (I did the first one for pitcher Sergio Romo (RM) to get you started). Note: All players were active (MLB) as of either 2021 or 2022.

RM (P) <u>R</u> <u>O</u> <u>M</u> <u>O</u>   SR (P) _ _ _ _ _ _   VLD (P) _ _ _ _ _ _ _ _

MD (P) _ _ _ _ _   ST (OF)_ _ _ _   HR (P) _ _ _ _ _ _

CN (IF) _ _ _ _   HS (C) _ _ _ _ _ _

9. LEVEL: TRIPLE

WHAT'S THE CONNECTION? . . . Given nine "things you might see" at a MLB game randomly placed in a grid, can you find the three groups of names/objects that are connected AND explain why they are connected (common theme)? Here's a sample grid:

Bat	Usher	Catcher
Vendor	Shortstop	Ball
Right Fielder	Glove	Ticket Taker

GROUP 1 NAMES: THEME:
Bat, Ball, Glove   Game "tools"

GROUP 2 NAMES: THEME
Usher, Vendor, Ticket Taker   Non-field personnel

GROUP 3 NAMES: THEME
Catcher, Shortstop, Right Fielder   Positions

For your puzzler, the following is a grid of nine MLB player names. Get the names and themes correct, and your screeching gap-shot lands you on third with a stand-up **TRIPLE.**

Babe Ruth	Warren Spahn	Lou Gehrig
Juan Marichal	Hank Aaron	Chipper Jones
Buster Posey	Willie Mays	Derek Jeter

GROUP 1 NAMES: THEME:

_________ _________ _________   ________________________

GROUP 2 NAMES: THEME

_________ _________ _________   ________________________

GROUP 3 NAMES: THEME

_________ _________ _________   ________________________

WORD FIND - 300 WIN CLUB . . . How would you like a starting rotation consisting of Bob Gibson, Whitey Ford, Sandy Koufax, Pedro Martinez, and Robin Roberts? Not too shabby, you might say, which would be the understatement of the century! If the previous five hurlers were not available to your team, but you could acquire the likes of Juan Marichal, Catfish Hunter, Don Drysdale, Bob Feller, and Dizzy Dean, you still would be feeling very, very good!

The 10 previously named pitchers are all in the Hall of Fame. They all were superior pitchers, putting trepidation into the minds of most opposing players, managers, and fans. However, none of these pitchers won 300 games in MLB.

The "300-win club" is a special category among HOF pitchers. In addition to elite talent, one needs (or benefits from) a long career, injury avoidance, and a host of other factors. The Word Find below is comprised of pitchers that reached this elusive plateau. Note: Pitchers are listed by first initial and last name. For example, Randy Johnson is RJOHNSON.

Find the name in the puzzle.

Names can go in any direction.

Names can share letters as they cross over each other.

300 WIN CLUB

```
R F G Q G B J P C G O U N
D J S M Q L N J Y U I R O
C N O J A E X G O L T V S
M L Y H I D P N U N P C N
A G P K S E D F N F K X H
T R R P R O D U G Y F R O
H O Q R C S N K X R W Y J
E V Y P U W S P A H N E W
W E V T N O T L R A C S W
S C T G L A V I N E M K R
O O G A L E X A N D E R E
N R E V A E S T N A Y R N
I K N D F O N I L S G B E
```

CMATHEWSON	CYOUNG	DSUTTON	EWYNN
GALEXANDER	GMADDUX	GPERRY	LGROVE
NRYAN	PNEIKRO	RJOHNSON	SCARLTON
TGLAVINE	TSEAVER	WJOHNSON	WSPAHN

11. LEVEL: DOUBLE

RHYME TIME . . . Each clue leads to a 2-word answer that rhymes, such as FLAT BAT or BALK TALK. The numbers in parentheses after the clue give the number of letters in each word of the answer. For example, "short answer by HOF pitcher Blyleven" (4, 4) would be "curt Bert."

1. Upbeat or happy manager (7, 7) ____________ ____________

2. Tall, thin person hawking his souvenirs in the stands (7, 6)

   ____________ ____________

3. An umpire's loud call when a batted ball is not fair (4, 4)

   ____________ ____________

4. Moving runners from one base to the next base (5, 4)

   ____________ ____________

5. A "boring contest" to many non-baseball people (4, 4)

   ____________ ____________

6. Convent women having a good time at the ballpark (3, 3)

   ____________ ____________

7. Ballpark fan eating numerous frankfurters (3, 3)

   ____________ ____________

8. The pitcher stands near the middle of this (5, 5)

   ____________ ____________

9. Hotdogs and hamburgers are surrounded by this (3, 3)

   ____________ ____________

10. Aaron's mischievous tricks or stunts (5, 6) pl.

   ____________ ____________

12. LEVEL: MULTIPLE

WALK-OFFS . . . When recalling 9th or extra-inning hits that won games (called walk-off hits), the hitter and often the pitcher that gave up the walk-off hit, are remembered for a long time. A case in point is the 1951 NL winner-take-all game between the New York Giants and the Brooklyn Dodgers. The Giants' Bobby Thomson's 3-run Home Run (called "The shot heard 'round the world") off the Dodgers' Ralph Branca cemented both player's names in baseball history. While the losing pitcher (LP) is remembered, the winning pitcher (WP) is often forgotten (Larry Jansen was the WP).

For this puzzler, you are given four walk-off hits in World Series history. Your task is to name the <u>winning pitcher</u> in the games.

One correct answer earns you a **SINGLE**, two correct is a **DOUBLE**, three correct a **TRIPLE**, and, if you get all four answers correct, you deserve a slow trot around the bases (**HOME RUN**).

1. The 1960 World Series ended when Pittsburgh's Bill Mazeroski homered off New York's Ralph Terry in the bottom of the 9th inning of game-7. As of 2022, this is the only World Series game-7 to end on a walk-off home run. Who was the winning pitcher for Pittsburgh?   ______

   a. Roy Face   c. Fred Green
   b. Harvey Haddix   d. Wilmer Mizell

2. In the 1993 World Series, Toronto's Joe Carter took Philadelphia's Mitch Williams "deep" (Home Run), to win the 6-game series. Who was the winning pitcher for Toronto?   ______

    a. Duane Ward   c. Danny Cox

    b. Al Leiter   d. Dave Stewart

3. Game-7 of the 2001 World Series pitted the New York Yankees against the Arizona Diamondbacks for all the "baseball marbles." What is remembered by many about the game – in addition, of course, to the fact that Arizona was the winner and World Champion – is that Mariano Rivera uncharacteristically lost the game in the bottom of the 9th inning. But who, you might ask, was the winning pitcher in this classic World Series game?   ______

    a. Mike Morgan   c. Greg Swindell

    b. Curt Schilling   d. Randy Johnson

4. The longest game (as measured in innings played <u>and</u> time) in World Series history occurred on October 26, 2018. The 18-inning, 7-hour and 20-minute contest, ended when Los Angeles' Max Muncy drove a Nathan Eovaldi (Boston) pitch over the left-center field wall.* Who was the winning pitcher for Los Angeles? ______

    a. Kenta Maeda   c. Alex Wood

    b. Kenley Jansen   d. Ryan Madson

*The Red Sox had the last laugh, however, as they won the championship, 4 games to 1.

13. LEVEL: DOUBLE

SCHMIDT. . . This puzzler is called Schmidt because of the <u>first</u> and <u>last</u> letters in the last name of this Hall of Fame third baseman. As an example, if the challenge (or question) was to name a way a base runner can get to second base following a single. One answer is to "steal" second base. The first and last letters of **S**chmid**t** are "S" and "t" which are the first two letters of "**ST**EAL."

Or, assume the name provided in the puzzler was Pete **Rose**. If the question was to name a "type of pitcher," the answer would be **RE**LIEF since the first and last letters of **Rose** are the first two letters of "**RE**LIEF."

The category for this puzzler is fielding "gaffes, goofs, screwups, or failures" and the player names are:

<u>NAMES</u>	<u>ANSWERS</u>
1. Eduardo **ESCOBAR**	1. _________
2. Jeff **BAGWELL**	2. _________
3. Craig **BIGGIO**	3. _________
4. Rick **FERRELL**	4. _________
5. Bill **MAZEROSKI**	5. _________

Your job is to provide the answers based on the examples of using the first and last letters of the player's last name which are the first two letters of the answer.

14. LEVEL: DOUBLE

CHICKEN OR EGG? . . . Which came first, the chicken or the egg? There are many things in baseball as well as in day-to-day life that are assumed to be "forever." However, there was a beginning for everything even though the start of an event is often forgotten.

In this "chicken or egg" puzzler, your task is to rank four baseball events (1 – 4) that are taken for granted by most fans of the game. The historical <u>first</u> (earlier) event should be ranked #1 and the historical <u>last</u> (most recent) event should receive a ranking of #4.

Historical Event	**Rank: Earliest to Latest**
A. 1st radio broadcast of a game	_____
B. Last team (Red Sox) to integrate	_____
C. Play-off system to determine pennant	_____
D. Inaugural Hall of Fame class	_____

15. LEVEL: TRIPLE

WORD FIND AND HIDDEN MESSAGE . . . This puzzler is a word find with a twist. The "twist" is that embedded in the word find is a hidden message.

Follow the directions that are provided on the next page. Get the hidden message and cruise into third with a stand-up **TRIPLE**.

This puzzle is a word search puzzle that has a hidden message in it.

First find all the words in the list.

Words can go in any direction and share letters as they cross over each other.
Once you find all the words, then copy the unused letters starting in the top left corner into the blanks to reveal the hidden message.

ALLSTAR	BERRA	CATCHER	CHAMPION
HITS	HOMERS	MANAGER	MISSOURI
MVP	OUTFIELDER	RUNS	YANKEES

__ __ ' __ __ __ __ ; __ __ __ __ __ __ __ __

__ __ __ __ __

16. LEVEL: HOME RUN

WAY TO GO, BRO' . . . There have been many biological brothers in MLB. The DiMaggio (Joe, Vince, and Dom) and Dean (Dizzy and Paul) brothers are two that many baseball fans recognize. How many "brothers" (last name) that played in MLB can you name in one minute? Name 10 for the **Home Run** level (DiMaggio and Dean count in the 10).

DiMaggio   Dean

17. LEVEL: TRIPLE

MORE TRIVIA . . . This puzzler tests your knowledge of MLB "leaders" and "firsts." Get the following five questions correct and bask in the glory of hitting a stand-up **TRIPLE**.

1. Which player is the All-Time MLB "Games Played" leader? _____

    A. Hank Aaron   C. Carl Yastrzemski

    B. Pete Rose   D. Ty Cobb

2. All-Time MLB "Batting Average" leader (career)?   ______

    A. Ty Cobb   C. Tris Speaker

    B. Babe Ruth   D. Pete Rose

3. All-Time MLB "Runs-Batted-In" Leader?   ______

    A. Jim Rice   C. Ted Williams

    B. Babe Ruth   D. Hank Aaron

4. First Latino elected to Baseball Hall of Fame?   ______

    A. Tony Perez   C. Roberto Clemente

    B. Rod Carew   D. Orlando Cepeda

5. First player to earn $5 million/year?   ______

    A. Sammy Sosa   C. Alex Rodriguez

    B. Mark McGwire   D. Roger Clemens

18. LEVEL: TRIPLE

ANAGRAMS . . . The letters of each MLB player's <u>last</u> name in this list can be rearranged in multiple ways to form other words. I provide the name; your job is to come up with <u>one</u> or <u>two</u> anagrams of <u>all</u> the letters in the surname (last name) of the player. For example: The letters in the name "CASTRO" (Jason and many others) can be rearranged to spell "actors" (or "castor").

Solve these ten questions/anagrams in five minutes and you can rest while standing on third base with a **TRIPLE**. (Note: Hall of Fame players are indicated by an asterisk (*)).

1.   BERRA (Yogi)*　　　　_______

2.   GROAT (Dick)　　　　_______

3.   STRAW (Myles)　　　　_______

4.   GOSLIN (Goose)*　　　　_______

5.   KLEIN (Chuck)*　　　　_______

6.   MANUSH (Heinie)*　　　　_______

7.   ROUSH (Edd)*　　　　_______

8.   WALSH (Ed)*　　　　_______

9.   SUTTER (Bruce)*　　　　_______　_______

10. FRIEND (Bob)　　　　_______　_______

19. LEVEL: SINGLE

WORD FIND - STEALS . . . Players that are a threat to steal bases are a headache to defensives, particularly pitchers and catchers. Some MLB players excel at stealing bases with Rickey Henderson leading the way with 1,406 "swipes" in his 25-year career. Henderson's 1,406 steals is 468 more than the second place "base thief," Lou Brock.

Below is a Word Find with 15 of the top base stealers in MLB history. Find them all and you earned a ringing **SINGLE**. Note: The players last name is preceded by the initial of his first name.

Find the name in the puzzle.

Names can go in any direction.

Names can share letters as they cross over each other.

```
N  L  B  E  H  W  A  G  N  E  R  L
B  O  M  W  I  L  L  S  S  O  B  O
C  R  S  T  A  N  B  N  Z  R  L  S
A  I  N  R  Q  Y  M  V  O  R  E  M
M  W  O  A  E  Y  T  C  O  B  B  I
P  W  T  I  C  D  K  O  A  U  H  T
A  I  F  N  O  X  N  L  Q  R  T  H
N  L  O  E  L  X  R  E  F  A  E  W
E  S  L  S  L  Y  E  M  H  F  K  Y
R  O  K  M  I  K  P  A  D  R  L  J
I  N  Q  C  N  Y  O  N  I  X  O  N
S  X  X  B  S  N  A  G  R  O  M  J
```

BCampaneris	ECollins	HWagner	JMorgan
KLofton	LBrock	MCarey	MWills
ONixon	OSmith	RHenderson	TCobb
TRaines	VColeman	WWilson	

20. LEVEL: HOME RUN

ONE HUNDRED PERCENT TRIVIA . . . This puzzler is pure baseball trivia. If you can answer these five questions, you've earned your **HOME RUN.**[2] (Remember, all answers reflect the rules in place at the end of the 2022 season).

1. The maximum length of a MLB bat is: ______

    a. 50 inches   c. 42 inches
    b. 48 inches   d. 38 inches

2. The width of home plate is: ______

    a. 20 inches   c. 12 inches
    b. 15 inches   d. 17 inches

3. The MLB minimum distance (recommended) from home plate to the backstop is: ______

    a. 75 feet   c. 60 feet
    b. 90 feet   d. 100 feet

4. The minimum distance in MLB stadiums (constructed after 6/1/58) from home plate to the right- and left-field foul poles is:* ______

    a. 315 feet   c. 325 feet
    b. 340 feet   d. 310 feet

5. The minimum distance in MLB stadiums (constructed after 6/1/58) from home plate to the center field fence is:* ______

a.	410 feet	c.	405 feet
b.	400 feet	d.	415 feet

*Some clubs have been permitted to construct parks after 6/1/58 with dimensions shorter than those specified.

21. LEVEL: HOME RUN

LETTER TILES . . . This puzzler uses a scrambled message and your job is to unscramble it. The unscrambled message is a quote from Ricky Henderson.[3] The quote is on 24 "tiles" which includes Henderson's name at the end (last four tiles).

For example, the scrambled message of "Baseball is a great game," might look like this (on seven tiles):

a gr	game	Base	e a t	.		i s	ball

The unscrambled message is:

Ba se	b a l l	is	a gr	e a t	game	.

Remember that four letters or spaces are on each tile.

Now, it's your turn to unscramble the Ricky Henderson quote.

Note: Remember, the quote uses four letters or spaces on each tile.

Unscramble the tiles to reveal a message.

Each tile is used only once.

Use spacing, punctuation and common words to find adjacent tiles.

Some words may be split into two lines.

n ' t	b a s	h a v e	m y u	n d e r	e t d	g i n	n i f o
m e . "	i r t y	' t g	, I	a n y	r m d	y H e	R I c k
s o n	t h i n	e b a l	d o n e	o e s n	t h e	l g a	" I f

22. LEVEL: DOUBLE

GOOD ARMS . . . This is a puzzler where you match a pitcher with the team (a – j) he is most associated with.

Note: Many pitchers (all players in general, and more so after free agency) played for numerous teams but the individuals in this puzzler are typically associated with one team. For example, Hall of Fame pitcher Goose Gossage is typically remembered as a NY Yankee although he also pitched for the White Sox, Pirates, Padres, Cubs, Rangers, Giants, A's, and Mariners.

Match the pitcher with the team (a – j) he is most associated with.

1. Sandy Koufax   ____   a. Indians
2. Juan Marichal   ____   b. Phillies
3. Jim Palmer   ____   c. Yankees
4. Tom Seaver   ____   d. Dodgers
5. Warren Spahn   ____   e. Cardinals
6. Roy Halladay   ____   f. Mets
7. Steve Carlton   ____   g. Giants
8. Dizzy Dean   ____   h. Braves
9. Bob Feller   ____   i. Blue Jays
10. Mariano Rivera   ____   j. Orioles

23. LEVEL: DOUBLE

PLAYERS THEN MANAGERS . . . Many former MLB players became MLB managers after their playing days were over. Some were both a player <u>and</u> manager at the same time. Some managers held records as players or achieved managerial accomplishments that are often forgotten with the passage of time. The puzzler below includes three questions about former players who also managed in MLB.

A. Which of the following MLB managers led the National League in stolen bases in 1941 as a MLB player? (Hint: He won two World Series championships as a manager)

1) Bobby Bragan   2) Danny Murtaugh   3) Cookie Lavagetto
4) Gene Mauch   5) Bob Scheffing   6) Billy Jurges

B. Which of the following MLB managers led their league in batting average as a MLB player? (Hint: He was quite the "talker")

1) Joe Cronin   2) Lou Piniella   3) Dusty Baker
4) Harry Walker   5) Billy Hitchcock   6) Yogi Berra

C. Which of the following MLB managers (formerly MLB players) won the greatest number of World Series titles <u>as a manager</u> (as of 2022)? (Hint: The World Series titles/championships were with an AL team)

1) Aaron Boone   2) Mike Scioscia   3) Chuck Tanner
4) Lou Boudreau   5) Terry Francona   6) Bucky Dent

24. LEVEL: TRIPLE

FOLLOW THE STEPS . . . If you follow each direction precisely, you'll uncover the last part of this Willie Mays quote:[4] "I don't rate them…" Just remember to follow the instructions specifically as they are listed. If you get this puzzler on the first try, you've cleared the bases with a **TRIPLE**. (I've given you the first line.)

1. Without spaces between letters, and ignoring the apostrophe, write down: I DON'T RATE THEM.
2. Remove the first E.
3. Change the second letter to a J.
4. Change the seventh letter to the first letter in the capitol city of Indiana.
5. Change the third letter to U.
6. Change the fourth letter to the first letter of the Mariners home city.
7. Change the sixth letter to the eighth letter in the alphabet.

    1. I D O N T R A T E T H E M

    2. ______________________________

    3. ______________________________

    4. ______________________________

    5. ______________________________

    6. ______________________________

    7. ______________________________

    8. ______________________________

25. LEVEL: TRIPLE

MLB FACTOIDS . . . From managers to shortstops, attendance figures to triple plays, with on-base percentage thrown in for good measure, this puzzler is a test of your knowledge of MLB facts.

Get all the answers correct and slide into third base with a **TRIPLE**.

1. The first full-time African American Manager in MLB.   ______

    A. Cito Gaston   B. Frank Robinson
    C. Ron Washington   D. Don Baylor

2. The Yankees were the first team to draw 1 million fans.[5]
    Name the year this event occurred.   ______

    A. 1920   B. 1930   C. 1940   D. 1950

3. Career On-Base % leader.   ______

    A. Ty Cobb   B. Barry Bonds
    C. Lou Gehrig   D. Ted Williams

4. This player has the distinction of hitting into the most triple plays
    (4) in MLB history.[6]   ______

    A. Ernie Lombardi   B. Ted Kluszewski
    C. Brooks Robinson   D. Mike Schmidt

5. Career leader in Double Plays turned as a shortstop.   ______

    A. Ozzie Smith   B. Derek Jeter
    C. Omar Vizquel   D. Cal Ripken Jr.

26. LEVEL: MULTIPLE

RHYME TIME . . . Each clue leads to a 2-word answer that rhymes, such as HIGH FLY. The numbers in parentheses after the clue give the number of letters in each word of the answer. For example, "A long home run by center fielder and All-Star Mike T. (5, 5)" would be "Trout clout."

1 – 2 correct:	You were robbed of a hit by a great catch.
3 – 4 correct:	**SINGLE**
5 - 6 correct:	**DOUBLE**
7 - 8 correct:	**TRIPLE**
9 - 10 correct answers:	**HOME RUN**

1. A shrewd or clever Machado (infielder) (5, 5) ________

    ____

2. Outfielder Betts in a very scary Halloween costume (6, 6)

    ________ ________

3. Salsa for ballpark nacho's (4, 3) ________ ________

4. Towering pop-up to outfield (4, 3) ________ ________

5. Ricky Henderson and Lou Brock had these (5, 4) ________

    ____

6. Umpire's loud call when base runner is NOT safe (3, 5)

    ________ ________

7. Pitcher Gerrit (his first name) scoring in soccer (4, 4) ________

    ____

8. Home team victory at Target Field (4, 3) _________ _________

9. Boisterous stadium (4, 5) _________ _________

10. Inexpensive game tickets (4, 5) _________ _________

27. LEVEL: MULTIPLE

SEEING DOUBLE . . . What do Carl **Hubbell** and Andy **Pettitte** have in common regarding their <u>last</u> name? I suppose linguistics and others would discover many similarities like both names are pronounced with two syllables, both names begin with a consonant, and others. However, for purposes of this question, both names of Hubbell and Pettitte have two pairs of double letters, i.e., two "b's" and two "l's" in Hu<u>bbel</u>l, and two sets of "t's" in Pe<u>ttitt</u>e.

How many other MLB players can you list <u>in three minutes</u> that contain two pairs of double letters in their last name? Counting Hubbell and Pettitte, three names (you only have to come up with one), and you stepped to the plate and lined a **SINGLE** to the outfield. Four names qualifies for a **DOUBLE**, and five names means you scampered all the way to third with a stand-up **TRIPLE**. If you can name six or more double-letter MLB players in three minutes then you can round the bases (proudly!) with a **HOME RUN**!

Remember, Hubbell and Pettitte count in your total!

<u>Hubbell</u>, <u>Pettitte</u>, ____

____

____

28. LEVEL: TRIPLE

ANIMAL DETECTIVE . . . This puzzle could be aptly named "sentence sleuth with animals." Hidden within the following 10 sentences – and all sentences contain one or more animals – are objects or events that you would likely see on the <u>ball field</u> of a MLB game. Ignore anything you might see in the grandstand, press box, luxury suites, etc.

The correct answer could be spread over one, two, or several words. All punctuation, capital letters, etc., should be <u>ignored</u> when searching for the hidden object or event. For example, the sentence: [Open woodlands, savannahs, and vast plains are suitable habitat for caribou, tigers, lions, and giraffes.] contains an event at a ball game. Do you see it? [Open woodlands, savannahs, and vast plains are suitable habitat for carib<u>ou, t</u>igers, lions, and giraffes.]. Note: "out" is the correct answer.

Can you find the hidden MLB object or event in the following sentences? Eight (8) or more correct and cruise into third with a **TRIPLE**.

Ten of these 20 game events or objects are the answers to questions:

Ball, base, bat, box, cap, catch, dirt, flag, grass, line, path, pitch, plate, pole, pop, run, safe, slide, strike, wall.

1. The small zoo had a large female bear with her cub, a llama, and four elk. _______________

2. The cougar, under the rock ledge, had found an ideal hiding place. _______________

3. Sarah saw a crab, a seahorse, and six urchins while scuba diving. ______________

4. The cockpit chairs were uncomfortable, making it difficult to stay focused on counting deer herds. ______________

5. The weasel, in early to its den, settled down for a long winter's nap. ______________

6. The big "cat" - cheetah - was lying in wait for the young deer. ______________

7. The large shrub oxen slept behind was an ideal hiding place. ______________

8. The hippo, leopard, and eagle exhibits were new additions. ______________

9. A rule for all zookeepers to follow – never disturb a tiger when it's sleeping. ______________

10. The alpaca, panther, and elephant were the zoo's most popular animals. ______________

29. LEVEL: DOUBLE

ANAGRAMS WITH A TWIST . . . This puzzler not only tests your baseball acumen but your knowledge of the English language as well. The six sentences below contain two blank spaces that must be filled in to make the sentence make sense. The "twist" however is that the words must be anagrams of each other (all letters of the first word must be used in the second word). For example, "The batter **flied** out to the deepest part of the **field**," contains "flied," and one of its anagrams, "field."

Now it's your turn. Getting all answers correct earns you a ringing **DOUBLE**. Note: The numbers after the blanks indicate the number of letters in the word/anagram.

1. Even though the "___(2) steal" sign was given, the runner grinned when proudly standing ___(2) third base.
2. A ___(3) on the back and a ___(3) on the player's shoulder were the coach's sign for the runner to steal second base.
3. The visiting team wore their traditional ____(3) stripes but they quickly donned jackets due to the ____(3) in the air.
4. The visitors rally was a real ____(3) punch but when the home team was victorious in extra innings, many fans felt a ____(3) on their heartstrings.
5. The catcher's ______(4) of hitting four home runs in the game, sealed the ______(4) of the losing team.
6. The speedy baserunner ______(5) the pitcher into a move ______(5) a balk by the home plate umpire.

30. LEVEL: TRIPLE

HIDDEN NAMES . . . This puzzle involves finding a last name of a MLB player (active in 2022) that is hidden somewhere in the sentence. The correct answer could be spread over one, two, or several words. All punctuation, capital letters, etc., should be ignored when searching for the hidden name. For example, the sentence: [Taking care of a herd of llamas and alpacas troubled the farm family] contains the last name of MLB player, Jason CASTRO (or other Castro's active in MLB in 2022 –

Miguel, Harold, Willi, etc.). Do you see the hidden name? [Taking care of a herd of llamas and alpa<u>cas tro</u>ubled the farm family].

Can you find the hidden MLB player names (last names) in the following sentences? A few of the sentences have clues for a specific player.

1. Etiquette and grammar teach lessons that will stay with teens throughout their lives. ____________ (clue: outfielder)

2. The "leader" on his horse and the "pack" burro, moved slowly up the mountain. ____________

3. Marsha, who refused to eat her meals, was anorexic. ____________

4. The only co-ed housing on campus was Franklin dormitory. ____________ (clue: shortstop)

5. The "Grandpa Gang" banner saluted a group of male runners over the age of eighty. ____________

6. The company president gave his imprimatur nervously to the manual. ____________

7. The 2-hour break gave Sam a chance to either listen to classical music or read his favorite novel. ____________

8. The Boy Scouts' airplane on the tarmac had optimism and enthusiasm in the cabin. ____________ (clue: infielder)

9. The pope named our bishop to a Vatican post. ____________ (clue: shortstop)

10. The Duke and Duchess were an elegant couple on the dance floor, regal-looking as always. ____________

YES OR NO? . . . The Infield Fly Rule, and its interpretation, can be for many a troublesome rule to apply correctly. The questions below are courtesy of Michael Morse and his *Baseball Brainteasers*[7] book. Get all the questions correct – Yes or No answers – and scoot into third with a TRIPLE. (Note: The umpire must "call" an infield fly [activating the rule]. Assume that in "Yes" answers, the umpire made the infield fly rule call, and in "No" answers, the call was not made.)

1. The bases are loaded with one out when the batter hits a high pop up to the infield. The shortstop cannot hold onto the ball when the third baseman crashes into him. Is this an "infield fly (rule)" even though the ball was dropped?

   Yes ___No ___

2. Last half of the 9th inning, two outs, and the home team is trailing. But runners are on 1st and 2nd base when the batter hits a high pop up in the infield. Is the correct call the "infield fly rule," making the game automatically over?

   Yes ___No ___

3. In the 10th inning, the score is tied, and there are no outs. The home team has men/women on 1st and 2nd base, and the batter tries to advance the runners with a sacrifice bunt. However, the batter executes the bunt poorly and pops up to the catcher in fair territory. Is the correct call the "infield fly rule?"

   Yes ___No ___

4. With runners on 1st and 2nd base and one out, the batter hits a high fly ball to shallow right field. The second baseman settles under the descending ball, but at the last second he slips on the wet grass, loses his balance, and watches the ball hit the ground. When the runners see the ball hit the ground, they advance to second and third. Is this an "infield fly" even though the ball landed in the outfield?

Yes ___ No ___

5. The bases are loaded with one out when the batter hits a high pop up to the infield. The shortstop cannot hold onto the ball when the third baseman crashes into him. The pitcher picks the ball up and throws to the catcher who is standing on home plate <u>before</u> the runner from 3rd base crosses the plate. Is this an "infield fly?"

Yes ___ No ___

Bonus: Is the runner from 3rd base out or is he/she safe at home?

Out ___ Safe ___

WHAT'S THE CONNECTION? . . . Given nine MLB player names randomly placed in a grid, can you find the three groups of names that are connected AND explain why they are connected? Here's a sample grid:

DAVID ORTIZ	DUKE SNIDER	BILL MAZEROSKI
WILLIE STARGELL	TONY CONIGLIARO	JACKIE ROBINSON
PEE WEE REESE	CARL YASTRZEMSKI	RALPH KINER

GROUP 1 NAMES:
Ortiz, Conigliaro, Yastrzemski

THEME:
Red Sox

GROUP 2 NAMES:
Reese, Snider, Robinson

THEME
Dodgers

GROUP 3 NAMES:
Stargell, Mazeroski, Kiner

THEME
Pirates

Here is the grid for you to ponder. Get the names and the themes correct, and 'Kiss It Goodbye." Your blast cleared the fence for a **HOME RUN**.

Ted Williams	George Brett	Ryne Sandberg
Cy Young	Nolan Ryan	Ernie Banks
Don Drysdale	Mookie Betts	Roberto Clemente

GROUP 1 NAMES:

______ ______ ______

THEME:

______

GROUP 2 NAMES:

______ ______ ______

THEME:

______

GROUP 3 NAMES:

______ ______ ______

THEME:

______

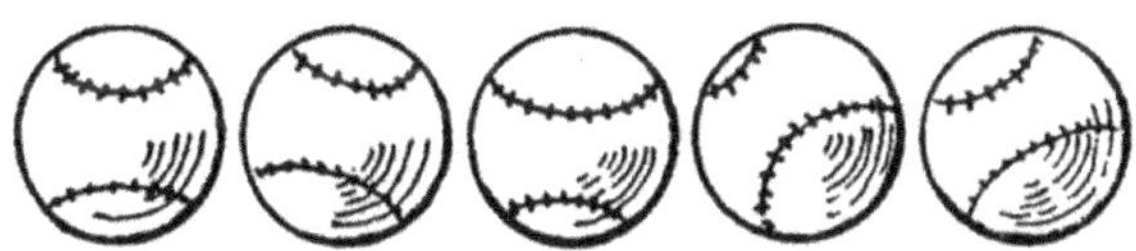

LATE INNINGS ANSWERS

1.

1. g	6. m
2. h	7. d
3. n	8. b
4. i	9. c
5. a	10. f

2.

BATTING AVERAGE CHAMPIONS

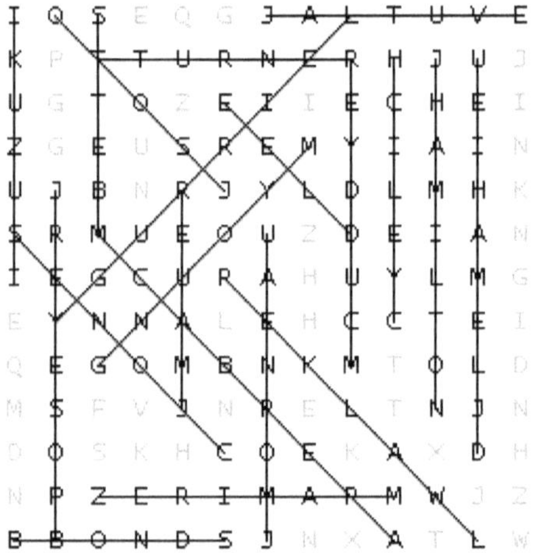

BBONDS	BPOSEY	CJONES	CYELICH
DJLEMAHIEU	DLEE	ISUZUKI	JALTUVE
JHAMILTON	JMAUER	JMORNEAU	JREYES
JSOTO	LWALKER	MBETTS	MCABRERA
MCUDDYER	MRAMIREZ	MYOUNG	TTURNER
YGURRIEL			

3.

There are many correct answers. The following is simply a sample.

1. Nolan Ryan O'Neal	Julio Franco Harris
2. Joe Morgan Freeman	Carlos Lee Trevino
3. Josh Harrison Ford	Fred Lynn Swan
4. Pee Wee Reese Witherspoon	Bill Terry Bradshaw
5. Shane Spencer Tracy	Dick Allen Iverson

4.

There are many correct answers. The following is a list of NL and AL stars who played in the 20th and 21st Century, and were elected to the Baseball Hall of Fame.

1. Aaron, Alexander, Alomar, Aparicio, Appling, Ashburn, and Averill.
2. Bagwell, Baines, Baker, Bancroft, Banks, Beckley, Bench, Bender, Berra, Biggio, Blyleven, Boggs, Bottomley, Boudreau, Bresnahan, Brett, Brock, Brouthers, Brown, Bunning and Burkett.
3. Campanella, Carew, Carey, Carlton, Carter, Cepeda, Chance, Chesbro, Clarke, Clemente, Cobb, Cochrane, Collins, Combs, Connor, Covelski, Crawford, Cronin, and Cuyler.
4. Davis, Dawson, Dean, Delahanty, Dickey, DiMaggio, Doby, Doerr, Drysdale, and Duffy.
5. Eckersley and Evers.
6. Faber, Feller, Ferrell, Fingers, Fisk, Flick, Ford, Fox, Foxx and Frisch.

5.

The "pattern" substitutes the letter in the alphabet <u>before</u> each letter in the clue.

The message is: <u>Three NL All-Stars in 2019: Anthony Rendon, Pete Alonso, and Freddie Freeman.</u>

6.

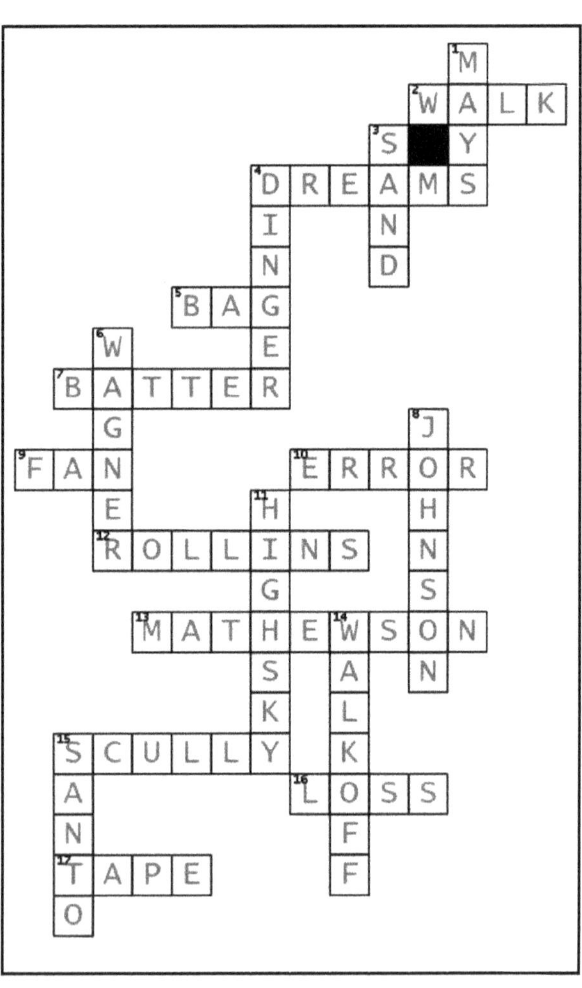

7.

Here is a sample name tower for the letters LA. Your tower will likely be different.

1.	LAU	Charlie, (1956-1967)
2.	LAMB	Jake, (2014-2020)
3.	LAIRD	Gerald, (2003-2015)
4.	LARKIN	Barry, (1986-2004)
5.	LAZZERI	Tony, (1926-1939)
6.	LANDRITH	Hobie, (1950-1963)
7.	LANCASTER	Les, (1987-1993)
8.	LAVALLIERE	Mike, (1984-1995)
9.	LAFROMBOISE	Bobby, (2013-2015)
10.	LANDENBERGER	Ken, (1952-1952)

8.

Romo, Soria, Eovaldi, Maeda, Soto, Heuer, Cano, Haase.

9.

Note: You may have grouped the names differently, but still correctly. The grouping below is merely one possibility.

GROUP 1 NAMES: THEME:
Ruth, Gehrig, Jeter   Yankees (predominately)

GROUP 2 NAMES: THEME
Spahn, Aaron, Jones   Braves (predominately)

GROUP 3 NAMES: THEME
Marichal, Posey, Mays   Giants (predominately)

10.

300 WIN CLUB

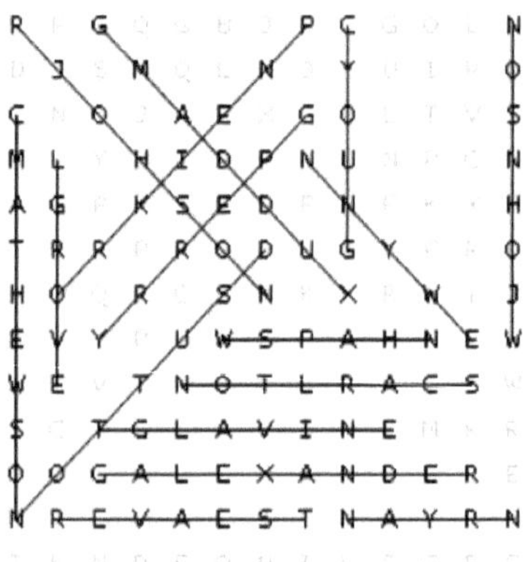

CMATHEWSON	CYOUNG	DSUTTON	EWYNN
GALEXANDER	GMADDUX	GPERRY	LGROVE
NRYAN	PNEIKRO	RJOHNSON	SCARLTON
TGLAVINE	TSEAVER	WJOHNSON	WSPAHN

11.

There are multiple correct responses to many of the questions. Here is one set of answers.

1. chipper skipper
2. slender vendor
3. foul howl
4. small ball
5. lame game
6. nun fun
7. dog hog
8. round mound
9. one bun
10. Hank's pranks

12.

1. b   2. a   3. d   4. c

13.

    1. Error   4. Flub

    2. Blunder   5. Miscue/Misplay/Mistake

    3. Boot/Bobble

14.

A. **1** (1921) https://baseballhall.org/discover-more/stories/baseball-history/voices-of-the-game

B. **3** (1959) https://www.mlb.com/news/players-who-broke-color-barrier-for-every-team

C. **4** (1969) https://www.baseball-reference.com/postseason/

D. **2** (1936) https://baseballhall.org/about-the-hall

Note: All sites were accessed on April 17, 2022

15.

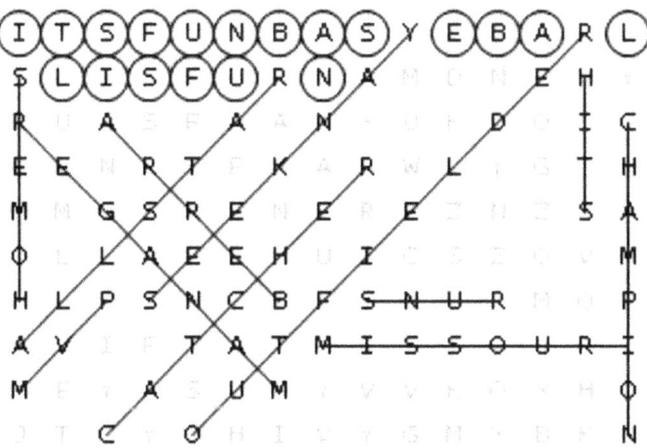

ALLSTAR	BERRA	CATCHER	CHAMPION
HITS	HOMERS	MANAGER	MISSOURI
MVP	OUTFIELDER	RUNS	YANKEES

I T ' S   F U N ;   B A S E

B A L L   I S   F U N

Hidden Message is: IT'S FUN; BASEBALL IS FUN.

16.

This list provides a few of the many brothers that played MLB.

Nola (Aaron & Austin), **Molina** (Yadier, Bengie, & Jose), **Alomar** (Sandy & Roberto), **Boone** (Bret & Aaron), **Alou** (Felipe, Matty, & Jesus), **Torre** (Joe & Frank), **Upton** (B.J. & Justin), **Hairston** (Jerry & Scott), **Weaver** (Jered & Jeff), **Izturis** (Cesar & Maicer), **Drew** (Stephen, J. D., & Tim), **Nettles** (Craig & Jim), **Brett** (George & Ken), **Cruz** (Hector, Tommy, & Jose), **Crespo** (Cesar & Felipe), **Sherry** (Norm & Larry), **Martinez** (Pedro & Ramon), **Waner** (Paul & Lloyd), **Perry** (Jim & Gaylord), **Boyer** (Ken, Clete, & Cloyd), **Niekro** (Phil & Joe), **Aaron** (Hank & Tommie), **Ripken** (Cal Jr. & Billy), **Maddux** (Greg & Mike), and more.

17.

1.	B.	Pete ROSE (3,562)
2.	A.	Ty COBB (.3662)
3.	D.	Hank AARON (2,297)
4.	C.	Roberto CLEMENTE (1973)
5.	D.	Roger CLEMENS (1991)

18.

1. rebar (or barer)	6. humans
2. gator (or argot)	7. hours
3. warts	8. shawl
4. losing (or logins)	9. utters, truest
5. liken	10. finder, redfin (or refind)

19.

Stolen Base Leaders

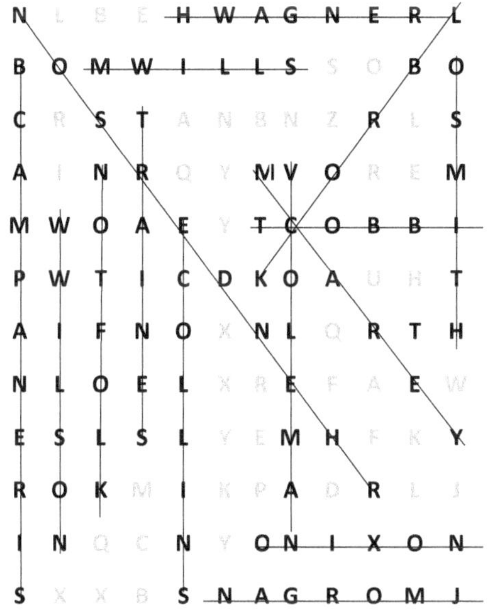

BCampaneris	ECollins	HWagner	JMorgan
KLofton	LBrock	MCarey	MWills
ONixon	OSmith	RHenderson	TCobb
TRaines	VColeman	WWilson	

20.

    1. c   2. d   3. c   4. c   5. b

21.

n ' t	b a s	h a v e	m y u	n d e r	e t d	g i n	n i f o
m e . "	i r t y	' t g	, I	a n y	r m d	y H e	R i c k
s o n	t h i n	e b a l	d o n e	o e s n	t h e	I g a	" I f

" I f	m y u	n i f o	r m d	o e s n	' t g	e t d	i r t y
, I	h a v e	n ' t	d o n e	a n y	t h i n	g i n	t h e
b a s	e b a l	l g a	m e . "	R i c k	y H e	n d e r	s o n

22.

1. d		6. i
2. g		7. b
3. j		8. e
4. f		9. a
5. h		10. c

23.

A. 2 – Murtaugh had 18 steals in 1941 to lead the NL.

B. 4 – Walker lead the NL in batting average (and all baseball) in 1947 with a .363 average.

C. 5 – Francona had 2 World Series titles – both with Boston in 2004 and 2007.

24.

The first part of Mays's quote: I don't rate them…" The second part is:

1. I D O N T R A T E T H E M

2. I D O N T R A T T H E M

3. I __J__ O N T R A T T H E M

4. I J O N T R __I__ T T H E M

5. I J __U__ N T R I T T H E M

6. I J U __S__ T R I T T H E M

7. I J U S T H I T T H E M

8. **I JUST HIT THEM**

25.

1. B (Frank Robinson—1975)
2. A (1920 —1,289,422 fans)
3. D (Ted Williams—.4817)
4. C (Brooks Robinson—4)
5. C (Oscar Vizquel—1,734)

26.

1. Canny Manny
2. Spooky Mookie
3. Chip Dip
4. High Fly
5. Fleet Feet
6. Out Shout
7. Cole Goal
8. Twin Win
9. Loud Crowd
10. Nice Price

27.

The following is a sampling of two pairs of double letters in past and present MLB: ZiMMMermaNN, KiriLLoFF, LiTTeLL, ABBoTT, WoRReLL, BuRReLL, MiLLwOOd, FeRReLL, SteNNeTT, GeNNeTT, SpliTTorFF, RuSSeLL, TaNNehiLL, TeBBeTTs, WaDDeLL, GuLLeTT, GaRReTT, CaNNizeRRo, CaNNeLL, PhiLLiPPe, TaNNehiLL, ABBatiCChio, MeRRiTT, SaLLEE, HeRRmaNN, and many more.

28.

1. . . . her cu**b, a ll**ama, and four elk.	ball
2. . . . couga**r, un**der. . .	run
3. . . . cra**b, a se**ahorse. . .	base
4. . . . cock**pit ch**airs. . .	pitch
5. . . . wease**l, in e**arly to its den. . .	line
6. . . . "**cat**" – **ch**eetah. . .	catch
7. . . . shru**b ox**en. . .	box
8. . . . hip**po, le**opard. . .	pole
9. . . . distur**b a t**iger. . .	bat
10. . . . alpa**ca, p**anther, and elephant. . .	cap

29.

The anagrams/answers are below but you may have a different pair of anagrams that also are correct.

1. no, on   4. gut, tug

2. pat, tap   5. feat, fate

3. pin, nip   6. lured, ruled

30.

Answers can have multiple responses (same last name for many players). Get the last name correct and the answer is correct!

1.	. . . gram**mar te**ach . . .	Sterling **Marte**
2.	. . . bur**ro, mo**ved . . .	Sergio **Romo**
3.	. . . wa**s ano**rexic.	Miguel **Sano**
4.	. . . Fran**klin dor**mitory.	Francisco **Lindor**
5.	. . . "Grand**pa Gang**" . . .	Emilio **Pagan**
6.	. . . imprima**tur ner**vously . . .	Trea **Turner**
7.	. . . musi**c or rea**d . . .	Carlos **Correa**
8.	. . . tar**mac had o**ptimism . . .	Manny **Machado**
9.	. . . po**pe na**med . . .	Jeremy **Pena**
10.	. . . re**gal-lo**oking . . .	Joey **Gallo**

31.

MLB states: An infield fly is any fair fly ball—not including a line drive or a bunt—which can be caught by an infielder with ordinary effort when first and second or first, second and third base are occupied, before two men are out.[8]

1. Yes
2. No, because there are already two outs. The game would have been over if the pop fly was caught.
3. No, since the "attempt" was a bunt and not a full swing.
4. Yes, there is no artificial boundary on an infield fly.
5. Yes, on an infield fly, the batter is automatically out, removing the force. In this example, the 3rd base runner is safe since he/ she was not tagged.

32.

Here is ONE example of a correct answer. You may have discovered another.

GROUP 1 NAMES: THEME:
Williams, Betts, Clemente   Outfielders

GROUP 2 NAMES: THEME:
Brett, Sandberg, Banks   Infielders

GROUP 3 NAMES: THEME:
Young, Ryan, Drysdale   Pitchers

[1] In addition to players, "others" included in the Baseball Hall of Fame are managers (i.e., Casey Stengel), umpires (i.e., Al Barlick), and executives (i.e., Branch Rickey).

[2] All answers from https://www.baseball-reference.com and https://www.mlb.com/glossary/rules (accessed October 28, 2022).

[3] https://www.justbats.com/blog/post/best-baseball-quotes-from-players-movies-more/ (accessed November 1, 2022).

[4] http://www.planetofsuccess.com/blog/2017/baseball-quotes/ (accessed December 21, 2021).

[5] https://www.baseball-almanac.com/teams/yankatte.shtml (accessed November 3, 2022).

[6] https://www.mlb.com/news/triple-play-threat-brooks-robinson-holds-infamous-mark/c-128131088 (accessed November 4, 2022).

[7] Michael A. Morse. *Baseball Brainteasers: 60 Major League Puzzles*. (New York: Sterling Publishing, 2006), 99 – 109.

[8] https://www.mlb.com/glossary/rules/infield-fly (accessed May 29, 2022).

4

EXTRA INNINGS

This is the most difficult chapter in the book (author's opinion). As an added (and optional) bonus incentive for the chapter, **Total Bases** can be computed for each question. Assign four bases to home run level questions that you correctly answer; and three for a triple, two for a double, and one for a single. Keep track of your **Total Bases**. Your optional "score" will be revealed at the end of the chapter.

1. LEVEL: TRIPLE

ALL STAR CROSSWORD . . . Since 1933, the top players in the AL and NL have squared off against one another in the annual All-Star Game. <u>Every</u> clue and answer in the crossword below pertains to this game, referred to by many as the "mid-summer classic."

Solving the crossword earns you a three-base hit (**TRIPLE**).

Use the clues on the next page to fill in the words.
Words can go across or down.
Letters are shared when the words intersect.

2. WINNING PITCHER OF FIRST ALL-STAR GAME

5. AL MANAGER FOR 2022 ALL-STAR GAME

6. NL MANAGER FOR 2022 ALL-STAR GAME

7. CAREER AT BATS

9. MOST TRIPLES IN ONE GAME

11. SINGLE GAME SLUGGING PERCENTAGE

12. MOST RUNS SCORED IN ONE GAME

13. CAREER GAMES STARTED AS A PITCHER (3 PLAYERS TIED)

15. CAREER BATTING AVERAGE (MINIMUM 25 PLATE APPEARANCES)

18. CAREER HOME RUNS

19. CAREER DOUBLES

20. GAMES PLAYED (3 PLAYERS TIED)

DOWN

1. CAREER SLUGGING PERCENTAGE (2 PLAYERS TIED)

2. WINNING PITCHER OF FIRST ALL-STAR GAME

3. CAREER SAVES AS A PITCHER

4. CAREER STRIKEOUTS FOR A PITCHER

8. MOST AT BATS IN ONE GAME

10. STATE WHERE 2022 ALL-STAR GAME WAS PLAYED

14. CITY THAT HOSTED FIRST ALL-STAR GAME

16. CAREER TRIPLES (2 PLAYERS TIED)

17. MOST HITS IN ONE GAME (3 PLAYERS TIED)

2. LEVEL: HOME RUN

GOT TRIVIA? . . . . The following five questions are a test of your MLB trivia knowledge. Get four (or five) of the answers correct, and "touch e'm all," for a booming **HOME RUN**.

1. Name the MLB player that got <u>exactly</u> a total of 3,000 career hits?

____

2. According to the Baseball Hall of Fame and Museum, this player is labeled as the "King of Foul Balls."[1] Can you name him? ______

      a) Luis Aparicio   d) Luke Appling

      b) Nellie Fox   e) Richie Ashburn

      c) Arky Vaughan   f) Willie Keeler

3. Sandy Koufax led the NL in strikeouts four times in the 1960s. Three of those years he struck out over 300 batters! Koufax also led the league in wins (3 years), shutouts (3 years), and earned run average (ERA) (4 years) during his time of dominance. He was elected to the Hall of Fame in 1972.

Here's a question for baseball trivia gurus: Where does Koufax rank in strikeouts compared to every pitcher who ever played MLB? _______

    a. 15th b. 51st c. 34th d. 24th e. 42nd f. 6th

4. Name the city and stadium/park/field where Babe Ruth hit the final Home Run (#714) of his career. ________________________________

5. Derek Jeter <u>grew up</u> in this state. _______

    a. California   b. Florida   c. Michigan
    d. New Jersey   e. Ohio   f. Pennsylvania

3. LEVEL: TRIPLE

FIRST NAMES—LAST NAMES . . . The <u>last</u> name of many MLB players is occasionally the <u>first</u> name of other people, sometimes famous "others." Below, a MLB player's first name (and clue) is provided. Your task is twofold: first, determine the player's <u>last</u> name which is also the <u>first</u> name of an "other," and then determine the last name of the "other" ("TV/Movie or Book Characters" and "Song Writers or Singers"). Make sure the players <u>last</u> name corresponds to the <u>first</u> name of the "other." Example: <u>Tommy John Steinbeck</u>, for the "others" category of

WRITERS. (Tommy John = Baseball player; John Steinbeck = Writer). I provided two answers to get you started. Solve this puzzler and end up on third base with a **TRIPLE**.

CATEGORY:
TV, Movie or Book Character

CATEGORY:
Song Writer or Singer

1. <u>Dale</u> <u>Murphy</u> <u>Brown</u>
   (Braves slugger who debuted in 1976; 2x MVP; 7x All-Star)

   <u>Gerrit</u> <u>Cole</u> <u>Porter</u>
   (Pitcher who debuted with Pirates in 2013; member of Yankees in 2022)

2. <u>Joe</u> _______ _______
   (HOF shortstop immortalized by _______ to Evers to Chance)

   <u>Alex</u> _______ _______
   (Long-time Royals outfielder; World Series champ in 2015)

3. <u>Jack</u> _______ _______
   (Played 18 seasons, first 10 with Giants; 340 career Home Runs)

   <u>Hank</u> _______ _______
   (HOF right-fielder; 755 career HRs; played 23 years in MLB)

4. <u>Jackie</u> _______ _______
   (Broke MLB color barrier)

   <u>Reggie</u> _______ _______
   (MLB career leader in strikeouts as a batter but also HOF member; 1973 AL MVP)[2]

5. <u>Mark</u> _______ _______
   (Slick fielding first baseman; 1988 Cubs debut; 16 years in MLB)

   <u>Tony</u> _______ _______
   (19 years in MLB, 15 with Phillies; 1958 debut; infielder; Cuban)

4. LEVEL: TRIPLE

Victor's Vowels . . . Victor is a sportswriter, but he has an aversion to the five vowels of a, e, i, o, and u. Victor drives his editor "bananas" due to his terrible spelling. Can you help his editor by inserting the vowels a, e, i, o, and u into the first two sentences of this story Victor filed? As a hint, the number of missing vowels in some words are indicated by the numbers in parentheses (); however, words NOT followed by a number still may have missing vowels.

Insert Victor's missing vowels correctly and pull into third base with a **TRIPLE**.

By wnnng th Strdy(3) ftrnn(4) clsh, th vctrs(5) lcl nn nrrwd(3) th pnnnt rc t thr gms t f frst plc. Th drdd(3) (nd htd) crss-twn rvls vst fr a fr gm srs(3) n Mndy.

____

____

_______________________________________.

5. LEVEL: HOME RUN

WHO'S ON FIRST? . . . . In 1938, the comedy team of Bud Abbott and Lou Costello performed a "wordplay routine" that can be found in the Baseball Hall of Fame and Museum. In fact, according to the HOF, the video of Abbott & Costello performing the "baseball-themed skit," is one of the Museum's most popular exhibits.[3] Titled "Who's on First?,"

Abbott, the straight man, portrays a manager, and Costello is an excitable player. Abbott comments that some players have strange nicknames, and his team is no exception with "Who" playing first base.

Can you provide the nicknames of other players on Manager Abbott's team?[4] Three names out of nine are provided to give you a "running start." Get three of the six remaining nicknames correct and you can do your **HOME RUN** trot.

1. Pitcher	D	A. Why	
2. Catcher	__	B. What	
3. 1st Base	G	C. Because	
4. 2nd Base	__	D. Tomorrow	
5. 3rd Base	__	E. Today	
6. Shortstop	__	F. I Don't Know	
7. Left Field	__	G. Who	
8. Center Field	__	H. (not mentioned)	
9. Right Field	H	I. I Don't Give a Darn	

6. LEVEL: HOME RUN

FOLLOW THE STEPS . . . If you follow each direction precisely, you'll uncover the last part of this Tony Gwynn quote: "Remember these two things . . . "[5] Below, I've given you the first line. Just remember to follow the instructions specifically as they are listed. If you get this puzzler on the first try, you've hit a **HOME RUN**.

1. Without spaces between letters, write down: REMEMBER THESE TWO THINGS

2. Eliminate the last four letters.

3. Switch the order of the fifth and 18th letters, the seventh and eighth letters, and the 11th and 16th letters.

4. Change the first T to an A, the second T to a V, and the third T to a U.

5. Change the first R to a P, first E to a L, the fifth E to a F, and the B to an A.

6. Change the third letter to A, eighth and 11th letter to D, and 18th letter to N.

7. Change S to eighth letter in alphabet, and first E to 25th letter in alphabet.

8. Change the second H to N, E to A, and, lastly, change W to the fifth letter in the alphabet.

    1. R E M E M B E R T H E S E T W O T H I N G S

    2. ____

    3. ____

    4. ____

    5. ____

    6. ____

    7. ____

    8. ____

    9. ____

(Could you complete the quote from Tony Gwynn?)

7. LEVEL: MULTIPLE

SEAVER AND RIVERA . . . David Devencio is a very strange fellow. David has many strange habits or quirks. One of these is his obsession with the letter "V," including MLB players whose last name contains a "V" (<u>not</u> a last name that begins or ends with a "V," but an "inside V"). Specifically, Tom Sea<u>v</u>er and Mariano Ri<u>v</u>era are two of his favorites.

How many MLB players, past and present, can you name in 3 minutes whose last name contains an "inside V" like Sea<u>v</u>er and Ri<u>v</u>era? You can include the two named in the last sentence to give you a head start.

If you name:
4 players or less in <u>3 minutes</u>, round first base with a **SINGLE**;
5 players, you just hit a **DOUBLE**;
6 players, and slide into third in a cloud of dust with a **TRIPLE**;
and 7 or more players, you hit a **HOME RUN**.

<u>Seaver, Rivera,</u> ____

____

8. LEVEL: HOME RUN

MATH . . . I hope you enjoy Math puzzlers. So, break out your pencils and paper, calculators, or other devices of your choosing. Get these two questions correct, and you just hit a **HOME RUN**.

1. The Dragons (visitors) were playing the Leopards (home team). Here are the innings when runs were scored:

- First inning: Dragons scored three runs but Leopards responded with two runs in their half of the first inning.

- Bottom of the third inning: 2^2 ("2 squared") runs were scored.

- Top of the sixth inning: π (pi) runs were scored (rounded to the nearest whole number).

- Seventh inning: Both teams scored one run.

- Top of the eighth inning: Square root of nine runs were scored.

- Bottom of eighth inning: Square root of four runs were scored.

- Reminder, all scoring in the game is shown.

- Questions for the puzzler: What is the Final Score (by Team) of the game?

Team____________   Runs______

Team____________   Runs______

2. Below are the pitches and their speed for Dragon's hurler "Fast
   Freddie."

   Fastball – 95 MPH
   Slider – 95% of speed of Fastball
   Curveball – 5% greater than speed of Change-Up
   Change-Up – 82 MPH

   Questions for the puzzler:

   What is the speed of "Fast Freddie's" slider? ______(in MPH)
   What is the speed of his curveball? ______(in MPH)

9. LEVEL: TRIPLE

ORDER, PLEASE! . . . Put the following list of six MLB players in order
of birth year, starting with the <u>youngest</u>. (Note: Place #1 by the
youngest, #2 by the second youngest, . . . with #6 by the oldest)

     __ Mike Trout   __Juan Soto

     __ Justin Verlander   __Freddie Freeman

     __ Jose Altuve   __Lance Lynn

10. LEVEL: HOME RUN

SPELLING BEE . . . This puzzler is a spelling, as well as a Hall of Fame
(HOF) player challenge. The letters on the outside of the (bee) hive can
be used as often as you wish (or not used at all) for a player's last name.
However, the middle letter must be used in the name.

For example, using the letters in the sample below:

The name "BANKS" can be found. Notice that the letter in the middle of the "hive" is used in the name (N). The name "AARON" can also be formed since the "N" is used, and the letter "A" is used twice. ("Anson" can also be formed. Cap Anson was a 19th century star, elected to the HOF in 1939).

Sample:

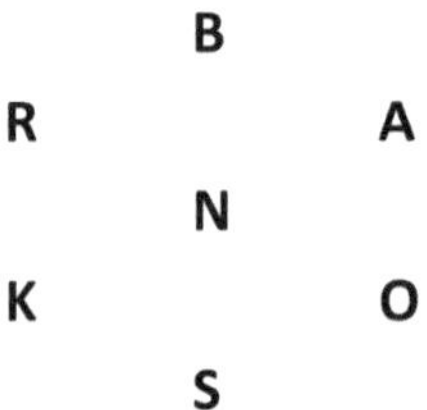

Now it's your turn. Can you find two Hall of Fame players in this "hive?" If so, circle the bases with a **HOME RUN**. If you can find three Hall of Fame players, your homer was a grand slam!

A
W   R
E
C   S
L

11. LEVEL: DOUBLE

NAME THE PLAYER . . . Many past players were known by a phrase or nickname that remained with them long after they retired.

This puzzle involves matching the phrase or nickname in the left column (#'s 1 – 10) with the player name in the right column (letters a – j). Eight (8) or more correct is worth a two-bagger (**DOUBLE**).

		(a-j)	
1.	The Sultan of Swat	____	a. Reggie Jackson
2.	Splendid Splinter	____	b. Pete Rose
3.	Yankee Clipper	____	c. Brooks Robinson
4.	Charlie Hustle	____	d. Dick Stuart
5.	Iron Horse	____	e. Willie Mays
6.	Mr. October	____	f. Babe Ruth
7.	Say Hey Kid	____	g. Ted Williams
8.	Mr. Cub	____	h. Lou Gehrig
9.	The Human Vacuum Cleaner	____	i. Joe DiMaggio
10.	Dr. Strangeglove	____	j. Ernie Banks

12. LEVEL: HOME RUN

BREAK THE CODE . . . Cryptograms are messages in substitution code. Break the code to read the message. For example, BABE RUTH might become ZYZC TSVJ, if Z is substituted for the B's, Y is substituted for the A, C for the E, and so on. (Note: Alphabet for cryptogram is a "continuing loop," i.e., A,B,C,...X, Y, Z, A, B, C,...X,Y, Z)

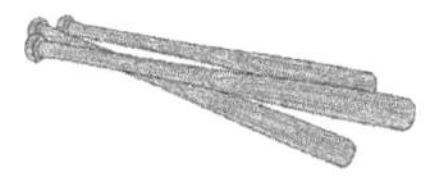

Can you break the code below? (Hint: Pay attention to <u>vowels</u> and <u>consonants</u> when breaking the code. The BABE RUTH example provides the "pattern.")

Uryl Osugyj md rfc Uyglr Jmsgu Eypbglyju fgr

20 rpgnjcu gl 1943 ylb 1946.

---- ------- -- --- ----- ----- --------- ---

20 _ _ _ _ _ _ _ _   _ _   1943 _ _ _   1946.

13. LEVEL: TRIPLE

REBUILD THE MESSAGE . . . This puzzler's hidden message (which includes the message's author) can be revealed by selecting a letter for each box or "cell" from the letters directly below the puzzle.

For example, the first cell contains a quotation mark ("). Note that no letters appear directly below the puzzle. The second cell has a "Y" and "I" below the puzzle. One of these letters must be placed in the second cell. Also, note that some cells already contain a letter or punctuation mark.

If you can rebuild the message, your game box score shows a **TRIPLE** for the plate appearance.

The letters from each cell are below the puzzle.

Try to rebuild the original message by choosing the letters for each cell.

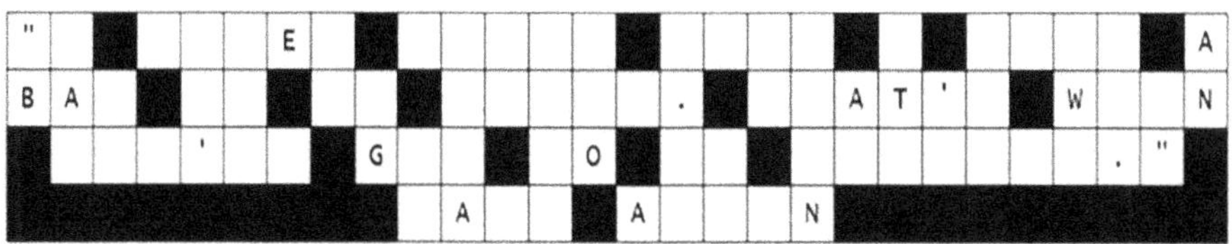

14. LEVEL: HOME RUN

TROUBLE IN PAIRS . . . It's two puzzles in one. First, unscramble the letters on each line to spell an English word (Ex: YPLSRAE unscrambled would be PLAYERS). Next, on the line <u>before</u> and <u>after</u> each unscrambled word, enter the first letter (on the left) and last letter (on the right). Then, unscramble the letters on the lines (go down each column) to reveal the last names of two baseball players. (Ex: for <u>P</u>LAYER<u>S</u> the P would be entered on the left line and the S would be entered on the right line; the P would be a letter contained in the <u>last</u> name of a MLB player, and the S would be a letter contained in the <u>last</u> name of another player).

NLGGNAI

(Hint: Another name for fishing)

— — — — — — — — —

IECWRRA

(Hint: In a plane's cockpit)

— — — — — — — — —

APTAALC

(Hint: Tree)

— — — — — — — — —

NOECBSE

(Hint: Disgusting or repulsive)

— — — — — — — — —

IMSALCU

(Hint: Melodius or harmonius)

— — — — — — — — —

RHLFAUM

(Hint: Damaging or injurious)

— — — — — — — — —

RBSITDU

(Hint: Interrupt or interfere)

— — — — — — — — —

15. LEVEL: TRIPLE

HOF VOWELS . . . This puzzler focuses on Hall of Fame players and the vowels (a, e, i, o, u) in their last name. As an example, A A _ O _ is a HOF player where three of the five letters in his name are vowels. Adding the two consonants of R and N completes the name of A A R O N (Hank Aaron). Another example is _ E _ E _. Adding the consonants of J, T, and R, spells the name of J E T E R (Derek Jeter).

For the seven HOF players on the next page, the vowels in their last names are provided. Your task is to insert the consonants to complete the name. Note: (1) All names are five letters in length, and (2) the first letter of the name is from <u>A through K</u> in the alphabet. Note: The "I's" in the puzzler are upper case "i's."

1. _ E _ _ A	Hint:	Catcher
2. _ I _ E _	Hint:	Feuded with Branch Rickey
3. I _ _ I _	Hint:	First MLB team was the Giants
4. E _ E _ _	Hint:	Starred for the Cubs
5. _ A _ _ _	Hint:	Infielder who was a Slugger
6. _ E _ _ _	Hint:	Catcher
7. _ _ E _ _	Hint:	Infielder who debuted in 1973

16. LEVEL: HOME RUN

BABE OR GEORGE? . . . Many, many decades ago (or as a famous person once said, "Four score and seven years ago…"), ball players often had nicknames (for first names) that became the "name" they were known by. "Babe" Ruth, "Dizzy" Dean, and "Lefty" Gomez are just three that went by their nickname rather than the name given at birth (George, Jay, and Vernon, respectively). In current times (or at least within the lifespan of most folks reading this question), nicknames are not as common for ball players, but they still exist. Below are the names of 10 MLB players (a few became MLB managers when their playing days ended). Do you know their birth (first) name? Get 7 of 10 names correct and you hit a "dinger" (**HOME RUN**). Note: Place the letter (a – j) on the line opposite the name (1 – 10).

1. Mookie Betts	______	a. Albert
2. Buster Posey	______	b. Daniel
3. Coco Crisp	______	c. John

4. Chipper Jones   _____   d. Markus

5. Sparky Lyle   _____   e. Harry

6. Tug McGraw   _____   f. Johnnie

7. Dusty Baker   _____   g. Covelli

8. Bud Black   _____   h. Frank

9. Rusty Staub   _____   i. Larry

10. Boog Powell   _____   j. Gerald

17. LEVEL: TRIPLE

BASEBALL TRIVIA CROSSWORD . . . A crossword is offered as your next puzzler. The crossword is baseball-related (it better be, you're probably thinking, since this is a baseball book!). Can you complete it? If so, you can proudly say, "I hit a **TRIPLE**."

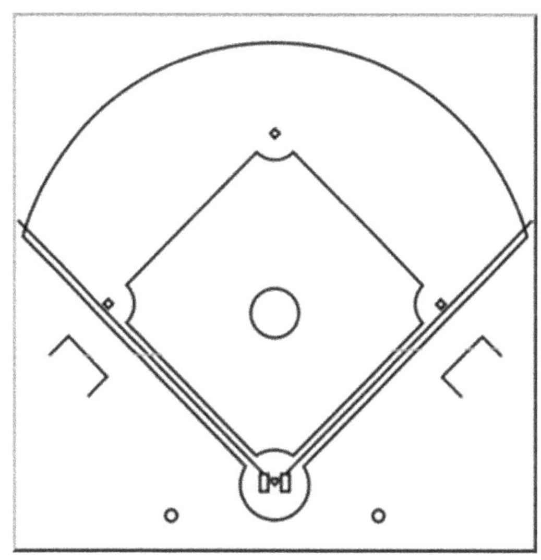

ACROSS

2. FIRST BASEMAN/OF WITH LAST NAME OF A "WINE" BRAND

3. RIGHT HANDED PITCHER WHO PLAYED MLB IN 2022

5. ANOTHER NAME FOR AN ARGUMENT

6. FORMER STADIUM OF DETROIT TIGERS

8. MLB MANAGER WITH FIRST NAME OF TERRY

10. MLB COMMISSIONER WHOSE FIRST NAME IS A CAR MODEL

11. ERNIE BANKS HAD THIS DISEASE IN 1963 (SALIVARY GLANDS)

12. "INVENTED" ANALYTICAL BASEBALL

13. MLB PITCHER TURNED BROADCASTER

14. FIRST BLACK MLB COACH

DOWN

1. BOTH WILLIAMS & MCCARVER (AMONG OTHERS) HAD LONG ONES

4. MLB PLAYER THEN NBA STAR

7. MLB PLAYER THEN "RIFLEMAN"

9. MLB PLAYER, MANAGER, AND GROUNDBREAKING G.M.

11. FAMILY OF CATCHERS

Use the clues to fill in the words below.

Words can go across or down.

Letters are shared when the words intersect.

18. LEVEL: MULTIPLE

HOME RUN TRIVIA . . . Four (4) players in MLB history hit home runs in their <u>teens</u> as well as in their <u>forties</u> (40+). All four players are in the list below (alphabetized).

<u>List of Players</u>

Home Run Baker, Ernie Banks, Don Baylor, Mark Belanger, Ty Cobb, Nelson Cruz, Julio Franco, Ken Griffey Jr., Rickey Henderson, Gil Hodges, Al Kaline, Tim McCarver, Stan Musial, Mel Ott, Wally Post, Tim Raines, Frank Robinson, Brooks Robinson, Alex Rodriguez, Babe Ruth, Gary Sheffield, Rusty Staub, Honus Wagner, Paul Waner, Ted Williams, Bill Virdon, and Carl Yastrzemski.

<u>Players named</u>	<u>Level</u>
One player correct:	**SINGLE**
Two players correct:	**DOUBLE**
Three players correct:	**TRIPLE**
All four players correct:	**HOME RUN**

Your answers:

____________________   ____________________

____________________   ____________________

19. LEVEL: HOME RUN

THE LETTER "E" . . . According to grammarians, etymologists, and others, the most common letter in the English language is E. To be more specific (for folks that care about such matters), the website English-Language-Thoughts states, "The letter [E] makes up 12.702% of the letters in an average text and is the most commonly-used letter in English."

Thinking of just Baseball Hall of Fame members with one "E" in their last name is relatively simple. For example, Lou GEHRIG is just one of many. A HOF member with two letter E's in their last name is a bit more challenging but still there are many: Harmon KILLEBREW and Tom SEAVER are two of the players.

However, three E's in the last name of HOF members (especially with 1901 as a career start date and excluding managers, executives, and umpires), is a short list of great players.

Can you name <u>three</u> HOF members (players) with three E's in their last name? (Hint — as of 2022, there was one pitcher, one infielder, one outfielder, and one outfielder/infielder, but your task is to only name three of them.)

____________   ____________   ____________

20. LEVEL: TRIPLE

RULES, RULES, AND MORE RULES . . . To many "casual" baseball fans, the rules of the game can sometimes be quite confusing. This is especially true of force plays ("...why doesn't the fielder have to tag the runner?..."), infield fly rule ("...what do you mean, the batter is automatically out?..."), sacrifice flies ("...how can a run score when the leftfielder caught the ball before it hit the ground?...") and other peculiarities of the game.

The following five situations don't happen very often, but they are a test of one's understanding of baseball rules (and definitely will impress the "casual" fan). Get all questions correct and end up on third base with an "impressive" stand-up **TRIPLE**.

1. The batter dribbles a slow roller down the third base line. The third baseman lets the ball roll, hoping it will go foul, since he has no play on the speedy batsman. Although the ball is in fair territory as it rolls down the line, it makes contact with a clump of dirt, and veers toward foul territory as it approaches the base. Then the ball grazes (touches) the third base bag and comes to rest in foul territory. Is this a fair or foul ball?[6]

   ____

2. The batter hits a line drive that strikes the pitching rubber and rebounds untouched into foul territory between home plate and first base. Fair or foul ball?[7]

   ____

3. With a count of 0-2, a pitched baseball bounces on home plate; however, the batter swings and misses, and the ball rolls to the backstop. Is the batter automatically out? Yes or no?[8]

____

4. The batter hits a high fly ball that is misjudged by the center fielder and bounces off his head and over the outfield fence. Is this a home run for the batter or an automatic double?[9]

____

5. The batter hits a high pop fly that bounces on the pitcher's mound (confusion among fielders as to who will catch the ball), and rolls into foul territory near home plate without ever being touched by a fielder. Is this a fair or foul ball?[10]

____

21. LEVEL: MULTIPLE

LOW AND INSIDE . . . This puzzler is called "low and inside" for the simple reason that a player's last name has the pronunciation "low" for one of the syllables, and "low" is "inside" the name. For example, Bartolo **Colon**'s last name has a "lo" pronounced "low," and is "inside" the name. (Mickey Lolich and Joey Gallo are incorrect answers however, despite their last names having the "low" sound. For Lolich and Gallo, the lo (low) is outside – first sound and last sound, respectively.)

For this puzzler, your challenge is to name MLB players (last names) where the letters "l" and "o" (pronounced "low") is "inside" the name. (NOTE: Last names must be unique, i.e., Bartolo Colon, Christian Colon, Roman Colon, Joe Colon, Cris Colon, etc., only count as <u>one</u> name.)

One "low" and "inside" name = **SINGLE**

Two names = **DOUBLE**

Three names = **TRIPLE**

Four names = **HOME RUN**

__________   __________   __________   __________

22. LEVEL: TRIPLE

RHYME TIME . . . Each clue leads to a 2-word answer that rhymes, such as FLAT BAT or BALK TALK. The numbers in parentheses after the clue give the number of letters in each word of the answer. For example, "a long home run by Center Fielder and All-Star Mike T. (5, 5)" would be "Trout clout." Eight or more correct earns you a **TRIPLE**.

1. Games after September 21 (4, 4) _____ ______

2. Kansas City player who spends entire career with his team (5, 5) _____ _____

3. Cobb's deceptive steal of home (3, 2) ______ ______

4. A very thin Minoso (6, 6) ______ ______

5. If former Cincinnati/Detroit manager contributed to "fake news" (6, 8) ______ ______

6. Meatless dinner for "Mr. October" (7, 7) ______ ______

7. Sacrifice by 1960s Mets second baseman (4, 4) ______ ______

8. An overweight "Louisville Slugger" (3, 3) ______ ______

9. A cheerful former Athletics reliever (5, 6) ______ ______

10. A batter's "under the weather" lumber (4, 5) ______ ______

23. LEVEL: HOME RUN

HOF VOWELS . . . This puzzler focuses on Hall of Fame players and the vowels (a, e, i, o, u) in their last name. As an example, O _ I _ A is a HOF player where three of the five letters in his name are vowels. Adding the two consonants of L and V completes the name of O L I V A (Tony Oliva). Another example is _ E _ E _. Adding the consonants of J, T, and R, spells the name of J E T E R (Derek Jeter).

For the seven HOF players below, the vowels in their last name are provided. Your task is to insert the consonants to complete the name. Note: (1) All names are five letters in length, and (2) the first letter of the name is from <u>L through Z</u> in the alphabet.

Hint: The last letter of the alphabet is contained in two of the seven names.

1. O _ _ I _
2. _ A _ _ O
3. _ O U _ _
4. _ E _ O _
5. _ _ O _ E
6. _ _ E A _
7. _ E _ E _

SCHOENDIENST . . . Red Schoendienst played in the major leagues for 19 years, mostly with the St. Louis Cardinals. "Red" debuted in the majors in 1945 with 1963 being his last season. He led the NL in fielding percentage six times and hit .300-or-better seven times. Red lead the NL in hits in 1957 (200), doubles in '50 (43), and stolen bases as a rookie (26). Schoendienst was a 10-time All Star and two-time World Series champion. He was elected to the Hall of Fame in 1989.

In addition to being a baseball great, the name "Schoendienst" is unusual. For starters, the name is not very common. Another reason for the unusualness is the length of the name (12 letters total).

Many common English words can be made from the letters in the name S C H O E N D I E N S T such as tone, code, need, etc. Notice (as an example) that there is only one "o" in Schoendienst so the word "tone" can be made but not "toon." Also, after making the word "tone," <u>all letters</u> are returned to the name Schoendienst and then the word "code" can be made.

How many <u>four or more</u> letter words (no plurals like tone<u>s</u> or code<u>s</u>) can you form from the letters in S C H O E N D I E N S T (with <u>replacement</u> of all letters after each word is formed)? There is no time limit on this puzzler! Note: Tone, code, and need, are three words that can be used in your count of "total words" found.

Up to 19 words: **SINGLE**

20 – 29: **DOUBLE**

30 – 39: **TRIPLE**

40 or more: **HOME RUN**

<u>tone, code, need,</u> ___________________________

____

____

25. LEVEL: HOME RUN

CHICKEN or EGG? . . . Which came first, the chicken or the egg? There are many things in baseball as well as in day-to-day life that are assumed to be "forever." However, there was a beginning for everything even though the start of an event is often forgotten.

In this "chicken or egg" puzzler, your task is to rank six baseball events (1 – 6) that are taken for granted by most fans of the game. The historical <u>first</u> (earlier) event should be ranked #1 and the historical <u>last</u> (most recent) event should receive a ranking of #6. Note: All historical events pertain to MLB. Also, get all correct, and your drive left the park for a **HOME RUN.**

Historical Event	**Rank: First to Last**
1. DH introduced in AL	a. ______
2. 1st night game	b. ______
3. 56-game hit streak	c. ______
4. 1st night World Series game	d. ______
5. 1st four consecutive HR's by four players on one team	e. ______
6. 1st MLB game in California	f. ______

TOTAL BASES OPTIONAL BONUS/INCENTIVE:

If you kept track of your **Total Bases** (TB) for the chapter, here's how you did:

65– 70 Total Bases   =   **Personal Record!**
Next year looks bright for you!

71 – 75 Total Bases   =   **Team Leader!**
Salary increase is in the future!

76 – 80 Total Bases   =   **League Leader!**
Clearly a top-level player!

81+   Total Bases   =   **MLB Leader!**
Congratulations! Maybe HOF someday!

EXTRA INNINGS ANSWERS

1.

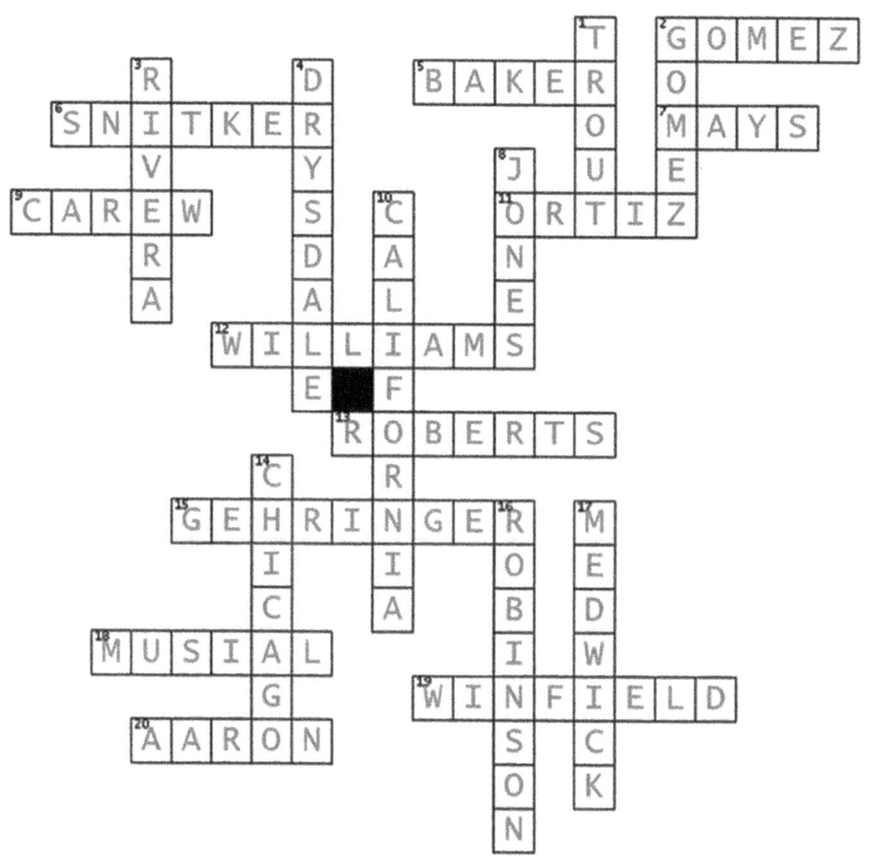

ACROSS

2   Winning pitcher of first All-Star Game . . . Lefty <u>Gomez</u> (same as 2 DOWN)

5.   AL Manager for 2022 All-Star Game . . . Dusty <u>Baker</u>

6.   NL manager for 2022 All-Star Game . . . Brian <u>Snitker</u>

7. Career At Bats . . . Willie <u>Mays</u> (75)

9. Most triples in one game. . . Rod <u>Carew</u> (2 in 1978)

11. Single game slugging percentage . . . David <u>Ortiz</u> (4.000 in 2004)

12. Most runs scored in one game . . . Ted <u>Williams</u> (4 in 1946)

13. Career games started as a pitcher . . . Robin <u>Roberts</u>, Don Drysdale, & Lefty Gomez (5)

15. Career Batting Average (min. 25 PA) . . . Charlie <u>Gehringer</u> (0.500)

18. Career home runs . . . Stan <u>Musial</u> (6)

19. Career doubles . . . Dave <u>Winfield</u> (7)

20. Games played . . . Henry <u>Aaron</u>, Willie Mays, & Stan Musial (24)

DOWN

1. Career Slugging Percentage . . . Mike <u>Trout</u> & Alfonso Soriano (1.000)

2. Winning pitcher of first All-Star Game . . . Lefty <u>Gomez</u> (same as 2 ACROSS)

3. Career saves for a pitcher . . . Mariano <u>Rivera</u> (4)

4. Career strikeouts for a pitcher . . . Don <u>Drysdale</u> (19)

8. Most At-Bats in one game . . . Willie <u>Jones</u> (7 in 1950)

10. State where 2022 All-Star Game was played . . . <u>California</u> (Dodger Stadium)

14. City that hosted first All-Star Game . . . <u>Chicago</u> (Comiskey Park)

16. Career triples . . . Brooks <u>Robinson</u> & Willie Mays (3)

17. Most hits in one game . . . Joe <u>Medwick</u>, Ted Williams, & Carl Yastrzemski (4)

2.

1. Roberto Clemente
2. d (Luke Appling)
3. b (51st)
4. Pittsburgh; Forbes Field
5. c (Michigan)

3.

1. Dale Murphy Brown   Gerrit Cole Porter
2. Joe Tinker Bell   Alex Gordon Lightfoot
3. Jack Clark Kent   Hank Aaron Copeland
4. Jackie Robinson Caruso   Reggie Jackson Browne
5. Mark Grace Kelly   Tony Taylor Swift

4.

By winning the Saturday afternoon clash, the victorious local nine narrowed the pennant race to three games out of first place. The dreaded (and hated) cross-town rivals visit for a four game series on Monday.

5.

1. D
2. E
3. G
4. B
5. F
6. I
7. A
8. C
9. H

6.

Gwynn's quote: "Remember these two things: <u>play hard and have</u> <u>fun</u>."

Here are the step-by-step answers to the instructions:

1. R E M E M B E R T H E S E T W O T H I N G S
2. R E M E M B E R T H E S E T W O T H
3. R E M E _H_ B _RE_ T H _O_ S E T W _E_ T _M_
4. R E M E H B R E _A_ H O S E _V_ W E _U_ M
5. _PL_ M E H _A_ R E A H O S E V W _F_ U M
6. P L _A_ E H A R _D_ A H _D_ S E V W F U _N_
7. P L A _Y_ H A R D A H D _H_ E V W F U N
8. P L A Y H A R D A _N_ D H _A_ V _E_ F U N
9. P L A Y   H A R D   A N D   H A V E   F U N

7.

Listed are a few of the names that contain an "inside V." Your answers will likely differ from the names below.

Seaver, Rivera(o), Alvarez, Altuve, Severino, Darvish, Musgrove, Duvall, Devers, Eovaldi, Ottavino, Weaver, Oliva, Lavagetto, Sandoval, Hargrove, Chavez, Garver, Grieve, Alvarado, Melvin, Deveraux, Davalillo, DaVanon, Popovich, Rivas, Pivetta, Avila, McCovey, Evers, Grove, Davis, Davidson, Colavito, Rivers, Alvis, Sturd(e/i)vant, Stevens, Stevenson, Sevcik, Taveras, Maranville, Irvin, Averill, Garvey, McCarver, Oliver, Javier, Givens, Donovan, Tovar, Cave, Graveman, Davenport, Kravitz, Savage, Lavarnway, LaValliere, Harvey, and many more.

8.

    1. Dragons 10, Leopards 9

    2. Slider speed = 90 MPH[a]

       Curveball speed = 86 MPH[b]

     [a] (0.95) x fastball speed of (95) = 90.25 (i.e., 95% of 95)

     [b] (1.05) x change-up speed of (82) = 86.1 (i.e., 105% of 82) or

       {[(.05) x 82] + 82}

9.

    1. Juan Soto (1998)

    2. Mike Trout (1991)

    3. Jose Altuve (1990)

    4. Freddie Freeman (1989)

    5. Lance Lynn (1987)

    6. Justin Verlander (1983)

10.

Rod CAREW

Pee Wee REESE

Joe SEWELL

11.

1.	f	6.	a
2.	g	7.	e
3.	i	8.	j
4.	b	9.	c
5.	h	10.	d

12.

The message is: <u>Stan Musial of the Saint Louis Cardinals hit 20 triples in 1943 and 1946.</u> The "pattern" substitutes the two letters in the alphabet <u>before</u> the vowels (a, e, i, o, u), and the two letters <u>after</u> the consonants.

13.

" I NEVER SMILE WHEN I HAVE A
BAT IN MY HANDS. THAT'S WHEN
YOU'VE GOT TO BE SERIOUS. "
HANK AARON

```
                    L

        V       SHNT       AEON        H

    YOUEV   M   OMIND   BHES   R   SUVH

    ITNINERYHTAKESWRTHEIIOASEE
```

14.

<u>A</u>NGLIN<u>G</u>, <u>A</u>IRCRE<u>W</u>, <u>C</u>ATALP<u>A</u>, <u>O</u>BSCEN<u>E</u>, <u>M</u>USICA<u>L</u>, <u>H</u>ARMFU<u>L</u>, <u>D</u>ISTUR<u>B</u>.

The players are Manny <u>MACHODA</u> and Jeff <u>BAGWELL</u>.

15.

1. Yogi BERRA   5. Ernie BANKS
2. Ralph KINER   6. Johnny BENCH
3. Monte IRVIN   7. George BRETT
4. Johnny EVERS

16.

1. d	6. h
2. j	7. f
3. g	8. e
4. i	9. b
5. a	10. c

17.

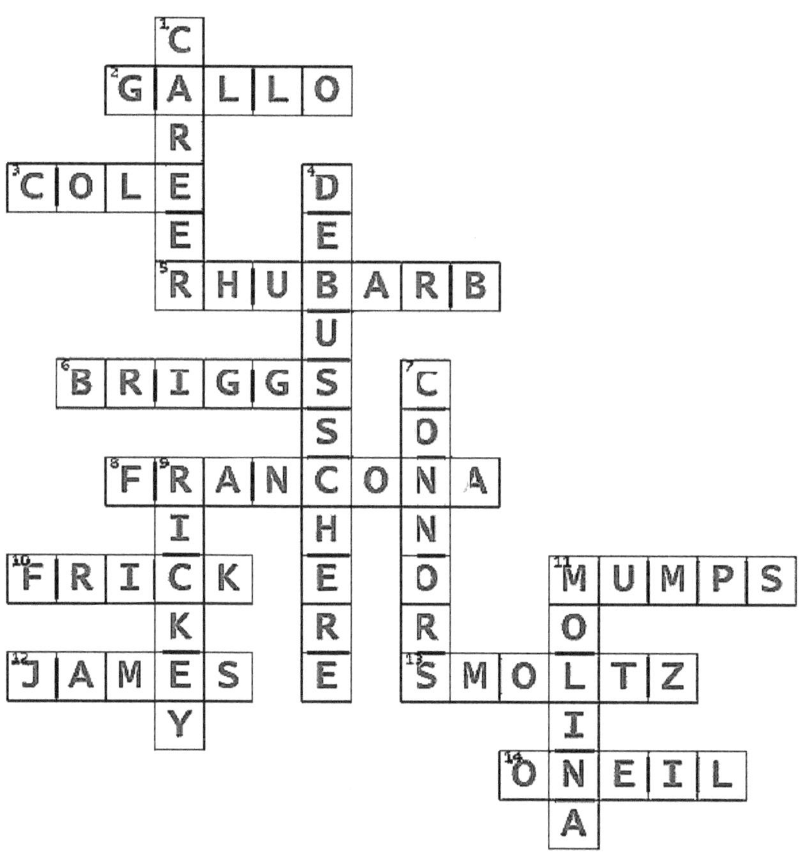

18.[11]

    Ty Cobb   Rusty Staub

    Alex Rodriguez   Gary Sheffield

19.

Any <u>three</u> of the four names are correct:

Roberto **CLEMENTE** (1955-1972); Hall of Fame 1973

Dennis **ECKERSLEY** (1975-1998); Hall of Fame 2004

Hank **GREENBERG** (1930-1947); Hall of Fame 1956

Pee Wee **REESE** (1940-1958); Hall of Fame 1984

20.

1. Fair
2. Foul
3. Batter is NOT automatically out and is allowed to run to first base.
4. Home Run
5. Foul

21.

These are possible answers. There are others. For your information, the years the individual played MLB is in parentheses (current as of the 2020 season).

Matt MALONEY (2009-2012)

Duane BELOW (2011-2013)

Kevin SLOWEY (2007-2014)

Roberto ALOMAR (1988-2004)

Heathcliff SLOCUMB (1991-2000)

Ron VILLONE (1995-2009)

Isaac GALLOWAY (2018-2019)

Brian SLOCUM (2006-2008)

Angel SALOME (2008)

Miguel DILONE (1974-1985)

Eddie SOLOMON (1973-1982)

Eddie MALONE (1949-1950)

Lefty SLOAT (1948-1949)

Bruce SLOAN (1944)

Hank MIKLOS (1944)

Mike MILOSEVICH (1944-1945)

22.

Your answers may differ from the ones below.

1. Fall Ball
2. Loyal Royal
3. Sly Ty
4. Skinny Minnie
5. Sparky Malarkey
6. Reggie's Veggies
7. Hunt Bunt
8. Fat Bat
9. Jolly Rollie
10. Sick Stick

23.

    1. ORTIZ, David

    2. SANTO, Ron

    3. ROUSH, Edd

    4. LEMON, Bob

    5. THOME, Jim

    6. WHEAT, Zack

    7. PEREZ, Tony

24.

The following is just a sampling of four-plus letter words that can be formed from the letters in SCHOENDIENST.

Chin, inch, echo, itch, cede, cent, code, coed, coin, code, dice, disc, hind, hint, hone, shed, shin, then, thin, dent, dine, done, hiss, hose, host, need, neon, nine, none, send, shoe, shot, tend, thee, this, diet, dote, edit, into, nest, nose, note, seed, seen, sent, teen, tide, tine, toss, chide, hence, chest, chess, ethic, cited, disco, scene, scent, tonic, sheen, dense, ethos, heist, snide, these, those, inset, noise, sense, stein, stone, tense, chosen, conned, stench, decent, cosine, insect, notice, honest, tendon, denote, sensed, tennis, tossed, contend, consent, descent, consist, diocese, dissect, section, dissent, intense, condense, indecent, and dishonest.

25.

a.	6^{12}	1973	AL
b.	1	1934	Phillies vs. Reds, 5/24/35
c.	2	1941	The 56-game Hit Streak by Joe DiMaggio
d.	5^{13}	1971	Orioles vs. Pirates, 10/13/71
e.	4^{14}	1961	Braves – Mathews, Aaron, Adcock, Thomas, 6/8/61
f.	3^{15}	1958	Dodgers vs. Giants, 4/15/58

- - **Extra Innings Endnotes** - -

[1] https://baseballhall.org/discover/luke-appling-king-of-foul-balls
(accessed April 19, 2023).

[2] https://sabr.org/bioproj/person/reggie-jackson/ (accessed April 27, 2023).

[3] https://baseballhall.org/discover/short-stops/whos-on-first (accessed November 21, 2022).

[4] James Buckley Jr. *The National Baseball Hall of Fame Collection: Celebrating the Game's Greatest Players.* (Bellevue, WA: Epic Ink, 2020), 77.

[5] https://www.justbats.com/blog/post/best-baseball-quotes-from-players-movies-more/ (accessed December 14, 2021).

[6] https://img.mlbstatic.com/mlb-images/image/upload/mlb/hhvryxqioipb87os1puw.pdf (accessed May 2, 2023). See "Definition of Terms."

[7] https://img.mlbstatic.com/mlb-images/image/upload/mlb/hhvryxqioipb87os1puw.pdf (accessed May 2, 2023). See "Definition of Terms, Comment after Foul Ball."

[8] https://img.mlbstatic.com/mlb-images/image/upload/mlb/hhvryxqioipb87os1puw.pdf (accessed May 2, 2023). See MLB rule numbers 9.12 (f) (2) and 9.13 (a).

[9] https://img.mlbstatic.com/mlb-images/image/upload/mlb hhvryxqioipb87os1puw.pdf (accessed May 2, 2023). See MLB rule numbers 9.12 (f) (2) and 9.13 (a).

[10] https://img.mlbstatic.com/mlb-images/image/upload/mlb/ hhvryxqioipb87os1puw.pdf (accessed May 2, 2023). See "Definition of Terms, Comment following Foul Ball."

[11] https://www.mlb.com/news/alex-rodriguez-homers-on-40th-birthday/c-139113372 (accessed December 14, 2022). Baseball Reference "appears" to also list Brooks Robinson as homering as a 19- and 40-year-old but his final home run was hit before his May 18 birthday so he was technically 39 years of age.

[12] https://www.baseball-almanac.com/firsts/teamdh.shtml (accessed January 7, 2023).

[13] https://www.baseball-almanac.com/ws/yr1971ws.shtml (accessed January 7, 2023).

[14] https://sabr.org/gamesproj/game/june-8-1961-milwaukee-braves-belt-a-record-four-consecutive-home-runs-in-one-inning/ (accessed January 7,2023).

[15] https://sabr.org/gamesproj/game/april-15-1958-giants-dodgers-meet-on-the-west-coast-for-the-first-time/ (accessed January 7, 2023).

- - BIBLIOGRAPHY - -

Books and Articles

James Buckley Jr. *The National Baseball Hall of Fame Collection: Celebrating the Game's Greatest Players.* Bellevue, WA: Epic Ink, 2020.

Julie K. Cohen and Amy Reynolds. *Baseball Puzzles: Brain Games.* Morton Grove, IL: Publications International, Ltd., 2010.

Nancy Linde. *399 Games, Puzzles & Trivia Challenges Specially Designed to Keep Your Brain Young.* New York: Workman Publishing, 2012.

Nancy Linde. *417 More Games, Puzzles & Trivia Challenges Specially Designed to Keep Your Brain Young.* New York: Workman Publishing, 2016.

Michael A. Morse. *Baseball Brainteasers: 60 Major League Puzzles.* New York: Sterling Publishing, 2006.

John Veneziano, ed. *Memories and Dreams,* 44(2) Lynn, MA: H.O. Zimman, Inc., 2022.

John Veneziano, ed. *National Baseball Hall of Fame and Museum: 2022 Yearbook.* Lynn, MA: H.O. Zimman, Inc., 2022.

Helpful Websites

Anagrams:

https://www.thewordfinder.com/anagram-solver/

Baseball Almanac:

https://www.baseball-almanac.com

Baseball Hall of Fame and Museum:

https://baseballhall.org

Baseball Reference:

https://www.baseball-reference.com

Major League Baseball:

https://www.mlb.com

Major League Baseball (Rules; General):

https://img.mlbstatic.com/mlb-images/image/upload/mlb/
hhvryxqioipb87os1puw.pdf

Major League Baseball (Infield Fly Rule):

https://www.mlb.com/glossary/rules/infield-fly

Puzzle Maker:

https://puzzlemaker.discoveryeducation.com

Helpful Websites

Society for American Baseball Research:

https://sabr.org

Word Find:

https://wordfind.com/

Word Tips:

https://word.tips/unscramble

Words (General):

https://www.merriam-webster.com

HALL OF FAME PLAYER INDEX

HALL OF FAME PLAYER INDEX

HALL OF FAME PLAYER INDEX

HALL OF FAME PLAYER INDEX

HALL OF FAME PLAYER INDEX

HALL OF FAME PLAYER INDEX

HALL OF FAME PLAYER INDEX

ACKNOWLEDGEMENTS

Where to begin? It's difficult to acknowledge all the folks that significantly helped me with this book, but I'll give it a try. My apologies to friends I may have overlooked; your contributions are also deeply appreciated.

First, I want to thank daughter Emily Bratkovich for giving me two books on puzzles, trivia, and challenges to keep one's brain young. These volumes were the inspiration that lead to the genesis of this book. Daughter Amy Erickson helped me with computer issues, clip art, and a host of other technical questions. Dad's love to both of you.

Numerous people reviewed book questions and answers, offered helpful suggestions, and served as a valuable sounding board to me. They include my brother Al Bratkovich and many others: Charlie Blinn, Rod Engelbart, Mick Gatens, Gene Gomes, Dan Levitt, Art Muligan, Stew Thornley, Phil Wolfe, and Rick Wriskey.

The folks at Story & Song Bookstore Bistro provided helpful counsel on publishing issues. In particular, my gratitude is extended to Donna Paz Kaufman and Luann Pollock.

Editing and formatting of the book, including the cover design, is the work of Carol Moses. Thank you very much!

And finally, my wife Janet. You served as my final copy editor, provided helpful guidance along the way, and put up with my "Puzzle Book" obsession. I Love You!

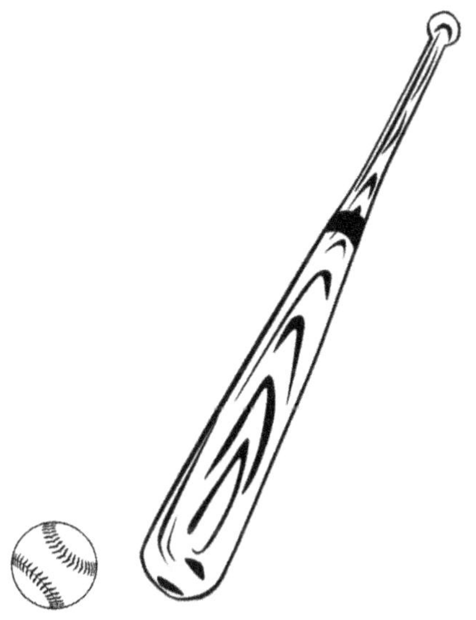